6/14

Almost A Wiseguy

Bob Puglisi

with

Vince Ciacci

DEDICATION

Dedicated to Danielle Ciacci

Also By Bob Puglisi

Railway Avenue

Almost A Wiseguy & Railway Avenue are also available as e-books

Table of Contents

BOB PUGLISI/VINCE CIACCI

AUTHOR'S NOTE

This is a memoir of Vince Ciacci's life as told to Bob Puglisi. Names of people and places have been changed for obvious reasons.

INTRODUCTION

I met Vince Ciacci in 1974, sitting at the pool of the apartment complex where we both lived in Hollywood. Since I grew up on the streets of New York with a similar Italian-American background, we had an instant rapport. There's a bond between New Yorkers no matter where in the world they meet, and when the ties are ethnic the bonds are even stronger. Vince told me he was a hairstylist, and eventually I went to him for haircuts. But there was more to this guy's story than I was aware of at the time. After that initial meeting, we'd spend Sunday afternoons drinking wine, sunning at the pool and talking about our pasts.

Growing up, we were close to our relatives, uncles, aunts and cousins who usually lived nearby. We were accustomed to big, delicious home cooked Italian dinners with the whole family. Our fathers were working stiffs; our mothers were housewives who were entrusted with our well-being and the cleanliness of our home. Our moms were a little neurotic, always complaining about one ailment or another.

Vince and I would often compare notes on our mothers' past and present ailments. Our parents were disciplinarians, and as children we would get screamed at or beaten with very little provocation. And since it was our mothers that were at home with us every day, it was they who would administer discipline most of the time. Our mothers' were feared, and they always held the "trump card" of "Wait 'til your father comes home," which couldn't be much worse than what we had already endured at our mothers' hands.

Even though our childhoods had many similarities, under the surface there was something very different about our lives. I did some things as a youth that I'm not particularly proud of, but as it turns out, my life was milquetoast compared to Vince's. Vince grew up wanting to be bad, wanting to be a criminal. As a teenager on the streets of Manhattan in the 1950s his motto was, "Live fast, die young, make a beautiful corpse," something he heard in the 1949 movie *Knock on Any Door*, starring John Derek as Pretty Boy Nick Romano. From the movie, Vince adopted the name "Nicky." Some people still know him as Nicky, and like Nicky Romano, Vince lived fast. Fortunately, he didn't die young. But by all accounts, he came close on many occasions. "Godshots," he calls them today. You might call them strokes of luck, miracles or divine intervention.

When I consider Vince's life, it reminds me that my life could have gone in a similar direction. Vince wanted to get in trouble knowing that it would hurt his parents. That's one of the ways in which our lives differ. Crime and evil deeds were his way of getting back at them for his terrible home life. I never wanted to embarrass my parents or to hurt them because I knew that they loved me. If I got in trouble, it was unintentional and usually the result of some stupid, thoughtless act. My biggest problem was going along with the crowd. I can't tell you how many times I heard that old cliché "If everyone jumped off the Brooklyn Bridge, would you do it too?" But this is Vince's story and I only point out the differences in our lives because Vince feels that his parents were at the core of why his life took the destructive path that it did.

Over the years, Vince confessed to me that he had done some dishonorable things and that he had been involved with the mob. But I couldn't begin to imagine the extent of his criminal activities. Then there were the alcohol and drugs that took over his life. I started drinking at the age of 14. It was just something you did with your friends, once again following the crowd. Vince started drinking at the unbelievably early age of five or six because it made him feel like a different person.

When I met Vince, I never thought of him as an alcoholic or a heavy drug user. Most of my Hollywood friends indulged in some sort of drugs. It was the '70s and doing drugs was perfectly acceptable behavior for people our age living in Hollywood. While I never saw Vince do any of these things, it also didn't seem like Vince drank more than I did. Maybe there were clues to Vince's addictions, but I was too slow to perceive them, or he was very good at hiding them.

During the process of putting this book together, I found out that Vince was an actor as a child and was in many school plays. Maybe that's how he kept his addictions hidden from friends and family. In fact, Vince never stopped acting. He used his acting skills during armed robberies to cover up his addictions and to mask his uneasiness around his mobster associates. Vince lived a double life: hairstylist by day, criminal, alcoholic, addict by night. Like me, most of his hairstyling customers never knew about this other life. He had done such a good job acting that when he finally confessed to his customers about his addictions, they were quite shocked and didn't believe him. To us he seemed a decent person, not what he was to his mob friends, where he had to put on a tough demeanor.

Throughout the years of our friendship, Vince and I shared many events: marriages, death of parents, baptisms, but there was always this other side of Vince that I knew very little about. I had seen some seedy characters that were his customers—L.A. Mafia guys whose hair he styled. He also had many friends from New York that had relocated to L.A. I always thought it amusing how their names all ended in a "y". There was Petey, Joey, Bobby, Tony, Vinny, Mikey... but I've also met some of his other customers and friends who were business professionals... doctors, movie studio executives, restaurateurs, and people from all walks of life. People naturally gravitate to Vince's charming personality. His stories and meticulous haircuts keep them coming back for more. Like me, many of his customers remain his close friends.

It wasn't until after the birth of his only child and the breakup of his third marriage that an unhappy Vince began to wrestle with his problems... alcohol and drug abuse, low self-esteem, crime and rage. It took some time before he confided in me that he was an alcoholic. I never really knew the full extent of his addictions until we started this book.

I wasn't the only one he talked to. There were other writers and people in the entertainment industry who were customers. They were always intrigued when he related stories about his life. They often told him they wanted to write about him, but those aspirations never materialized. For years, I urged Vince to sit down with me to write his life story. I would tell him many times my idea for the title *Almost A Wise Guy*. It wasn't until the summer of 2001 that he began to take me seriously.

In 1998, I moved to Colorado. Three years later I spent a lot of time in L.A., producing a short film that I had written. It was like old times sitting in Vince's barber chair again and listening to his stories. I finally convinced him to let me write his story. I felt honored when he consented. It meant he trusted me enough to confide his deepest secrets.

That summer he and his 13-year old daughter visited me in Colorado. We fished during the day and in the evenings after dinner, Vince and I sat on my front porch smoking fine cigars. I interviewed Vince and recorded the details of his life. At first, I was shocked by his story and felt like a voyeur. After his visit, I played back the tapes and still couldn't believe what I heard. I even asked him if he hallucinated while on drugs or alcohol. He swore on his mother's grave and his daughter's life that what he told me was the God's honest truth.

Vince was not a well-known crime figure who made headlines. He was just another soldier in the mob with aspirations of becoming a 'made-man.' He's remorseful about his past and hopes this book will be an inspiration to other people with similar problems. I had known my friend for close to thirty years, and even though I suspected certain things about him, they weren't even close to the real story that unfolds in this book.

CHAPTER 1

Coxsackie Reformatory

During the Korean War columnist Walter Winchell said, "If your son is in Korea, you send him a package. If your son is in Coxsackie, you send him a prayer." Coxsackie Reformatory in the Catskill Mountains of Upstate New York is where 18-year old Vince Ciacci served three-years for armed robbery. This is the same correctional institution were the boxer Jake LaMotta served time as a youth and subsequently learned how to box.

The 750-acres of fields and pastures that surround the institution are in the village of West Coxsackie (an Indian word for "hoot of an owl"), and located two miles west of the Hudson River and 23 miles south of Albany. There were no walls or fences and its ivy-covered red brick buildings give it the appearance of a prep school. A quarter mile, tree-lined boulevard divided by a grassy mall leads to the three-story administration building with its bell tower and weather vane. Coxsackie's principal buildings are built around a square courtyard. The administration and food service buildings are on the west and east sides of the courtyard. Two cellblocks on the south look across at two identical structures on the north. Behind the food service building is a long vocational training building. The six cellblocks that house inmates each have three floors with 42 cells on each floor.

Coxsackie is a totally self-sufficient vocational institution. On its farm, inmates grow their own vegetables and slaughter their own cows and pigs. Fresh milk and eggs are provided daily from their own dairy. Vince claims, "Everything that we ate up there was grown or raised there.

And to be honest, the food wasn't that bad. It ain't like Raymond Street Jail, the Brooklyn House of Detention, or the County Jail in L.A. where the food is terrible.

"When I was in Coxsackie, that's when I ran into real tough Italian guys." The guys Vince befriended at Coxsackie were from different parts of New York City and other cities such as Syracuse, Buffalo, Rochester and Boston. These people would have a significant influence on his future following his release.

As with most correctional institutions, Coxsackie had rules. It wasn't just the institution's rules; the inmates had their own rules. If you broke either the institution's rules or the inmates, you paid a desperate price either at the hands of the guards or the inmates, respectively.

The courtyard in the center of the buildings served as the recreation yard which was divided into what the inmates called pads. These pads were areas of turf occupied by specific groups of inmates that were cliques or gangs, usually segregated by race. The administration viewed this as a disturbing practice. Nevertheless, the prisoners diligently adhered to the rules concerning pads. If you went into some other group's pad without permission, it resulted in a beating from its inhabitants.

"It was all bullshit rules, but you had to follow them. We had our own clique of Italians called 'Good Boys' and we hung on the back wall. They were the worst of the worst. You got the Brooklyn Good Boys' pad, Manhattan Good Boys' pad. Next to Manhattan is a Queens' pad, then a Staten Island pad, and then you got the porch where the guard stays.

"After that on the other side of the yard, you got a Buffalo 'half-ass' pad, meaning they're bad guys but they're not as tough as we were. They're legends in their own minds. You got a Syracuse half-ass pad, and then you have a pad full of Bronx half-asses. They were very tough bastards even though they were half-asses. You had a pad of black guys called 'Mesopotamia' that were as bad as the Good Boys. They usta put handkerchiefs in their back pockets, blue and red, meaning you were looking for a 'rep,' and who do you look for to get a rep—the Good Boys. Those black guys and the Good Boys were the big gunslingers at Coxsackie. Next to them, there was this other black pad that were half-asses. Then you got the 'creep blacks' pad. Right in the yard guys would get behind them and do it to them. It was weird. That's how these guys paid to stay in their pad. They had no honor.

"Then, you went down a little bit, and there was another black pad. Then down on the corner, you had this kid, Petey Baldoni. There was a Polish guy that hung with him, Little Joe somethin' or other, a bad motherfucker. Oh, Petey'd 'go up' (start a fight) on anybody. He was a real pretty boy, too. Petey was always fightin', always fightin'. Then, next to Petey's pad, there was a pad that I owned, a half-assed pad. Then there was the Puerto Rican pad followed by a creep pad. You go another 30 feet and there were no pads, then came the Good Boy pads again.

"Yeah, I had property. If you had property in that joint, you were rich."

Vince didn't smoke. In fact, he was repulsed by the smell of cigarettes. But at the time, he was astute enough to know there was money to be made in the joint by selling cigarettes, and his cigarette business prospered. "I had cigarettes all over the place. I usta have 400 packs of cigarettes and you can only keep so much in your cell. So I'd give them to the creeps—I'd let them hold 20 or 30 packs. I had a good amount of money up there. The place was like a little organized crime syndicate. You had loan sharkin' and we usta gamble. We also had protection. Some guys didn't pay for protection, and they would pay the price by gettin' a beatin'."

The number one rule for going into a pad was simple: you don't go into another pad without permission. Each pad had its own imaginary borders that couldn't be crossed without permission from a member of that pad.

"All the Good Boys were friends, but if you're in Brooklyn Good Boys, and you wanna go inside another Good Boys pad, you gotta walk outside the pad and you gotta walk to the line of the other pad, and say somethin' like, 'Bobby!' And Bobby has to say, 'Come on in!' Then you can walk in. If you walk in and nobody invites you, you can be best friends with the whole pad, but whoever sees you first has to go up on you. That never happened when I was there. Out of all the fuckin' crazy shit that the 'moulinyans' (black guys) pulled, there's not one ever had the courage or the balls to run inta a Good Boy pad. That would'a been like a Kamikaze Pilot. But we did that to them. Oh, fuck yeah... me and Bobby Marini did it one time. It was insanity. It incited a riot. We were walkin' on the track, and I ran in with him. Oh, we got killed. Like 20 guys jumped us, then all the Good Boys came over, then we got killed by the guards. But that's the way it was. You could be a Good Boy and be friends with a half-ass, but you go to his pad and you don't walk inta the pad without permission."

Things were different in the dining room. It wasn't segregated the way the yard was. "You sit next to whoever you sit next to. You'd be next to a black guy, a Puerto Rican. Oh, yeah, they don't fuck with that, but you don't talk to a black. See if you're a Good Boy and a black guy's sittin' next to you, you don't talk to him. Sometimes you did. The rules got broken once in a while, but it wasn't cool. In the yard, you wouldn't be seen walkin' with either a creep or a black guy. A Good Boy could walk with a half-ass guy, a half-ass guy with a Good Boy. Even a half-ass guy with a creep if he knew him good, or he's tryin' to put the make on him or somethin', but you never see a black and white walkin' together.

"If a black guy would touch the meat in the kitchen, there was a 'wire' that went out and no one white would eat the meat that night because he touched the meat. Oh, that was ridiculous. Deep in my heart I thought it was kinda crazy 'cause I usta get hungry. When somebody'd say, 'There's a wire on the meat.' I'd say, 'Fuckin' great. I gotta eat potatoes tonight.' It was crazy. You know how many nights I went hungry 'cause of that, and I had to put out wires, too, 'cause eventually I worked in the kitchen. And we had to go by those rules. They were shit rules."

The biggest problem for Vince in Coxsackie was the fights he got himself into. They always resulted in extended periods of time in solitary confinement. "It was like hell 'cause I was always in fights."

As a member of the Manhattan Good Boys, Vince had friends that he could depend on and trust to 'watch his back'.

"The guy that I hung with was Bobby Marini. We were like partners. If Bobby got fucked up and he wound up in the hole, if he had a fight with a moulinyan, 'bood' or whatever we usta call them, we both wound up in the fight and in the hole.

"Some of the Good Boys who were my friends were 'Gravedigger', whose name was Ralphy Marceau. He wasn't even Italian, but he was a bad guy that hung with us on the back wall. And there was Tony Marino, Joey Marino, Bruno Marino. There were more Marinos up there than you wanna think about. There was Red the Mick who was an Irish guy. There was a guy named Mickey Matt, and a guy called Fat Nat who talked with a lisp. There was Ray Cool Boys from Boston; he was an Italian guy, too. There was Sally Paoloni. Sally was a crazy little Guinea fuck—always in trouble. He was a Brooklyn guy. And there was Johnny Goomba, John Surfella. 'Madone,' could this guy fight."

In the recreation room, tables were also segregated. "There was the Good Boy table, the half-ass table, the creep table, the moulinyan table and the Puerto Rican table. Well you don't sit at a table where you don't belong. So one day, Johnny Goomba was sittin' at the rec table by himself, some moulinyan came in—he was lookin' for a rep. He sat at the Good Boy table. Johnny jumped over the table. Not only did he beat the shit out of the moulinyan, he jumped over to the black table. There were two black tables. One was the Mesopotamia table—the badass black table. They weren't afraid of nobody, and they were Good Boy hunters. Meaning, they were looking for reps. Well Johnny jumped over that table and dropped four moulinyans—bam, bam, bam, bam. Knocked them out. They threw Johnny in the hole. Johnny was a legend at Coxsackie.

"Then there were the riots. The shit would hit the fan in the yard. I was involved in a couple of riots where some of my friends disappeared. They got beat up real bad by the guards. I think 'cause one or two of them 'went up' on a guard. And that's it, you go up on a guard in the joint—you're dead. They'd disappear and nobody'd ever heard from them again. Who knows what happened to them. It was always a mystery."

Vince also took his share of beatings at the mercy of the guards. "I got beat up by the 'hacks' pretty bad. But as far as like fights—I remember once I had a fight with this black guy. He cut my lip pretty good with his hands. But I pretty much won most of the fights up there. I hung out with a lot of really tough fuckin' kids. It was terrible how much I was in the hole.

"I wasn't in population for more than a month at a time, before I was thrown in the hole because I'd do somethin'—a fight, or somethin'. See I always had a lot to prove all the time. You know, in the movie *Goodfellows*, Paul Sorvino says to Ray Liotta, 'That kid Tommy—he's a good kid, but keep away from 'im. He's always got a lot ta prove.' That was me. I always had to prove myself, and I was still a very skinny guy. I was a real pretty boy, too, and there was nobody fuckin' this kid. So I was always fightin'. But once you got a rep up there nobody really fucked with you. But we wanted a bigger rep so we'd get inta fights and riots."

During Vince's three years he was in solitary confinement nine times. "They usta make a joke about it. And I usta love to fix my cell up with paintings and things on the walls 'cause it shows that you're somebody. If this guy's cell looks good, it means he's making money. If he's makin' money, he's with the right people. I'd set up my cell, a week would go I'd be so comfortable, and somethin' would happen—back in the hole. I was a fuckin' idiot. Believe it or not, the hole was up on the third floor of the administration building; they called it A3.

"Everytime you fuck up in the joint they got a court, and you go inta court."

The deputy superintendent headed this disciplinary court. The court considered disciplinary action as a corrective rather than as a punitive action.

"They'd look at your charge. You had a fight, or you had contraband. They'd give you 'strippo time.' They give you either a five-day 'strippo,' or if you really fucked up, they'd give you like five days strippo, and then they put you on what they called 'assign.' You'd be in the hole on a mattress at night. They take your clothes away. They keep you in a t-shirt and shorts. Or, if they really wanted to fuck with you, they'd get you in there naked. It was cold, too, and freezin' in the winter.

"And assign is like you're on the coal gang shovelin' coal summer or winter. You'd take the coal from one end of the yard to the other end of the yard, closest to the furnace. The guard runnin' it wanted it made inta a pyramid. It was just punishment—to break your spirit. You'd have to load all this coal in a wheelbarrow then you gotta run up a ramp, which was murder on your back and your knees, but I was young then. You get to the top of the ramp, and it levels off. Then you take it all the way to the end of the ramp and dump it. Then, you come down another ramp, and you start shovelin' coal in the wheelbarrow all over again. You do that over and over, five, six hours straight. (I got problems with my knees today, and I attribute that a lot to being on that coal gang.)

"If you fuck up when you're on the coal gang, you can get killed. I remember one time I had a fight with this black guy. He said somethin' to me, and I hit him with my shovel, and I went at him. I had to 'get my shit off' because the guard runs from the top with a baton, and he would have been on me in 20 seconds. So in 20 seconds I had to do a lot of damage to this black guy. Which I did and then they did a lot of damage to me. Yeah, I worked him over, and I got him. They threw me in strippo again. They kept me in there for five months.

"That time when I was in the hole, I heard guards come upstairs that first night. I knew what was gonna happen. I heard the door go 'clang,' and it opens and five guards run inta my cell with 'batons,' and they beat me. I wouldn't say a word, blood all over the place. You didn't hear a peep outta me. They hit me. I wanted to scream. I wanted to yell. They beat me and beat me. And I took the beatin' 'cause I wanted to be a tough guy. Yeah, right! And they leave you there. I thought I was dead. I kept goin' in and out of consciousness."

CHAPTER 2

My Not So Great Childhood

As a young child Vince's family fondly called him "Vinny the Angel." The name came partly from his mother Leticia's maiden name Angeli, and partly because Vince had an angelic face. Vince claims "Vinny the Angel" was a contradiction because he was far from being an angel.

His father Sebastian was a barber, a very good one according to Vince. His mother was a typical Italian-American housewife. While her husband cut hair to put food on the table, she cooked, cleaned, cared for the house, and took care of her son and mother—Vince's grandmother lived with them as well.

"Grandma was a good lady. Actually, she protected me when I was a kid from the insanity that was going on in the house. There was always a lot of screamin', yellin' and bullshit you had to put up with."

One of Vince's worse childhood memories is what his parents would do when the family would come over.

"My mother would put me in the middle of the room and they'd talk about me. Bad shit I did. 'And, he did this… He did that…' It doesn't do much for a kid's self-esteem. I loved my Aunt Olavia 'cause she never liked when they did that to me. She always stood up for me. She usta call me Junior. 'Aah, don't bother Junior. Leave Junior alone,' she would say. She loved me, that woman. 'Cause my mother and father were tyrants with that shit. They were bitter. I hated that shit. You know, to put your laundry out on the street like that. You take care of that privately."

Growing up was difficult for Vince in many ways. His parents never instilled in him any positive self-esteem, which affected how he related to everyone around him.

"My mother said that when she had me she almost died, and she told me she couldn't have any more kids. When I was a kid, I was very lonely. I would'a wanted a brother, even if he beat the shit out of me. It would have been nice to have an older brother or a younger sister—just somebody. But it never happened."

Until Vince was about two years old, his family lived in a tenement on McDougal Street in Greenwich Village. Vince feels that his parents moved out of Greenwich Village because of the violence created by the Genovese Crime Family who controlled lower Manhattan. The Genovese family was one of the five New York Mafia families that ruled the New York Metropolitan Area at the time. Their turf was "Little Italy." Little Italy consisted of Greenwich Village on the West Side of Manhattan and the East Village on the Lower East Side.

When Vince was born in 1941, Frank Costello was Godfather of the New York Mafia. It was the glory days of the mob, a life young street thugs aspired to. Eventually, even young Vince would be attracted to this glamorous life. The very neighborhood and the criminal element that his parents moved him away from as a young child is where Vince chose to make his friends and spend his time when he was older. The criminal activities his parents feared growing up in Little Italy would foster were the same ones Vince would gravitate to.

In the early forties, the mob was behind most illicit activities in the city. Its influence extended across the Hudson River and into New Jersey. But under Costello's rule there was a relative calm. Costello liked to work out disagreements without resorting to violence. Prior to that there were gang wars with shootings that left gangsters lying dead in the streets of Little Italy.

With these images etched vividly in their minds, the Ciaccis moved uptown to 51st Street and 1st Avenue on the East Side. Today, this is an upscale area of Manhattan know as Beekman Place.

"It wasn't that hot when I was living there. There were a lot of tenements on one side. It's funny, one side was like where the rich people lived, the other side was like the lower class and middle class working stiffs. The rich side had elevated apartments. Where I lived, there were no elevators—just walk ups."

The move uptown may have also been warranted by his father's desire to be closer to work. He had his own little barbershop in the Daily Mirror Building (a now defunct New York City daily newspaper) on 45th Street between Second and Third Avenues. Sebastian didn't pay rent for his shop.

"My father had a way of people doin' things for him. My father, for as little as he was, had a big set of balls. He was born in Italy, and he came here with all of his brothers when they were teenagers. There were five or six of them. They were a pretty tough bunch. One uncle was a boxer. One uncle was a wrestler. But my uncles were all straight-laced guys. I think when they came here they raised a little hell. But later on, they were all married and had kids, and not one of my uncles was dishonest.

"On 51st Street, we had a two bedroom apartment and my grandmother had one bedroom; my mother and father had the other bedroom, and I slept in the middle of the living room on a 'Castro Convertible.' I never slept well, and I was extremely nervous. They walked in and out of my room all the time. There was no privacy. Some kids put up pictures, or somethin' like that—not me. I couldn't put anything up on the walls in my room 'cause it was the livin'room."

Not only were his sleeping arrangements difficult, but he lived with the constant threat of violence both out on the street and at home. There was an incident with his parents when he was ten or eleven that he still remembers vividly.

His mother would make soup. When he didn't like it, and his parents weren't looking, he'd dash to the closest window and throw the soup out. The window happened to be over the airshaft separating the buildings. One evening after throwing the soup away, there was a knock at the door. It was a woman from downstairs. She complained to Vince's father, 'Somone's throwin' food out your window. Come down and see what a mess it is.'"

Looking suspiciously at her son, Leticia said to her husband, "Go look, Sebi."

Vince knew right away he was in trouble. His father went downstairs with the woman. He saw different colored soup stains splattered all over the walls and floor of the airshaft. He returned to the apartment and without questioning his son, took off his belt and beat Vince, warning him, "If ya ever do that again, ya'll get a worse beatin'."

On that occasion Vince knew exactly why he received a beating, but that wasn't always the case. Most times, he didn't know the reason his parents were hitting him.

"When I was a kid, my father was always disciplinin' me. I always was doin' somethin' wrong and he'd make me come down to the barbershop and sit there for hours 'til he wasn't busy. I found myself actually enjoin' watchin' him cut hair. I was fascinated with the way he cut hair. When he had time and wasn't workin' he would discipline me. He would tell me this, tell me that. But I always had to wait a long time to be disciplined."

Vince grew to resent all the discipline and control his parents had over his life.

"They had old-fashioned ideas about how to raise a kid and about discipline. It was always about being hit. I never felt love. All I knew was discipline, discipline, always discipline. You know I started doin' a lot of bad things 'cause of that. I felt like that kind of attention was better than no attention at all. They were showing affection in their own strange way.

"On the streets and in school, I was a troublemaker, too. I always started trouble with my friends 'cause they didn't really like me. I started fights, and I usta antagonize the older guys in my neighborhood until they'd catch me and beat me up. I had a weird way of thinkin' and doin' things when I was a little kid. I never felt like I really fit inta anythin'. I always felt different. I had some real peculiarities, too. I usta grind my teeth, twist my hair."

The obsessive-compulsive characteristics Vince possessed were not commonly understood at the time, especially by his parents who didn't know anything about them. In their minds, he was just a bad kid. Vince also claims he had Attention Deficit Disorder.

"They didn't know about that back then. Nobody knew nothin' then... I used to fuck up in school. I'd be in class... I couldn't concentrate. I'd be daydreaming, or worrying about how to get out of school without catchin' a beatin'. *How am I gonna get in my neighborhood without the older guys comin' after me? How was I gonna survive the night at home without gettin' beat up?* It was just chaotic. There was no fun. There was no pleasure. It was like a game of survival. I wasn't enjoying life."

Needless to say his parents did little to endear themselves to Vince when he would get into scrapes at school or on the street.

"I felt no loyalty for my mother and father. I didn't respect my father. You know I wanted my father to be somebody different. Like big and tall and a manly type... I mean he was a man. He was a tough little man. But he was a little man. And I guess I never really respected him as a man. He was fast with the hands—with the barber strap, with the yellin'. That was a big thing in my house: yellin' and screamin' all the time. I never felt like I had a happy childhood. I lived in a controlled environment. Whatever my parents decided they wanted to do, they dragged me along. That went on up 'til about 12 years of age."

At his parents' hands, Vince experienced total humiliation and he had to endure it. So to avoid feelings of inadequacy, and the life he was forced to live, Vince started drinking at an unbelievably young age. This became the foundation for the problems that would plague his adult life.

"My mother usta have these big parties with lots of Italian food... antipasto, chicken soup with little meatballs, lasagna or macaroni with meat in the gravy, Italian pastries and everything. She'd have all the relatives over. It was back in the day when children should be seen and not heard. Children got in the way. I had three or four cousins about the same age. We were kids together. When they grew up, some of them hung around with the wrong people and got in trouble, too. And it all started as little kids tryin' to get attention from their mothers and fathers, and their parents telling them, 'Go... Go 'way. Get outta here. Go do somethin'. Leave us alone.'

"That's the way it was when we were growin' up. I remember when I was five, six, my cousins and I, when nobody was lookin', we'd sneak a drink because they always had liquor on the tables. We'd drop an unfinished drink real fast. You'd have three, four of those at five, six, seven years old, you'd get floatin'. From then on, I knew if I drank it made me feel like somebody different."

CHAPTER 3

I Wanna Be A Hoodlum

Growing up, Vince was a skinny little kid. As a result, he got pushed around a lot by the bigger tougher kids in school and in his neighborhood. "When I was a kid, I always usta watch cowboy movies and wanted the bad guy to win; the bad guy dressed in black with crisscrossed guns strapped to his legs. I always had this feeling inside me for drama, for the dangerous side of life."

Vince's transition from being pushed around to being the one doing the pushing took place one afternoon when Vince was around 14 years old.

"We went to see this movie with Marlon Brando, a whole bunch of us from the neighborhood, *The Wild One*." This 1954 movie starred Brando as the leader of a motorcycle gang that terrorizes a small town.

"We all went crazy for that movie. After we left the movie, we decided we were gonna buy black leather jackets and boots [black motorcycle boots]. The only problem—it wasn't just a style with us. We wanted to become bad kids."

At that young age, Vince and his friends were already shoplifting on a regular basis.

"We'd go into markets, candy stores, department stores. I mean any place that we could go where we could steal. I don't know why we did it. Maybe it was that I wanted stuff. It was the excitement of it. It was bad. See, I figured it this way—when I was real little—I was so good and I got hurt for it. I tried to be a nice kid and I got pushed around at home, at school and on the street. Then, when I got older and started pushin' back, I started to get respect. It was a negative type of respect, but I sorta thrived on it. That movie jump-started my criminal career. It put something bad in me."

But it took a fistfight with a neighborhood bully to start a series of life-changing events for Vince that would ultimately end up with his serving time at Coxsackie.

"This guy usta pick on me all the time... Italian guy named Louie Di Marco. We were down in the park. He pushed me and fucked with me, and I just turned around and hit him with a left hook and he went down. I hit him the first time, and I saw what I did with that punch. I was a skinny kid so it was as much a surprise to me as it was to him and everyone else. When I saw him fuckin' crumble to his knees, I just got on top of him and it was like all the years of being pushed around came to a head. I just tore him up; tore him up. I just beat him half-ta-death."

When the older guys in the neighborhood saw the damage Vince had done to this older and bigger kid, they asked him, "Did you do that?"

From that day on Vince began to realize that he could be one of the tough kids in the neighborhood.

"All those years I was scared and holdin' back. But then all that fright sorta turned into rage and anger and it just exploded. That was when the trouble really started. That was the dividing line for me. When I crossed that fine, thin line, I wanted it all."

Another incident in 1958 cemented Vince's tough guy image.

"I was at a dance at the YWCA on 53rd and Lex."

At the dance, Vince met a girl named Virginia, a raven-haired beauty with a great shape, who would become his first girlfriend.

"I'm dancin' with Virginia and these guys started some shit. They said somethin'. I said, 'Fuckin' guys! Who the fuck are you guys?' I wasn't fightin' with them, but I told them, 'You come here next week, ya mother fuckers—ya bring whoever ya gotta bring, and ya fuckin' be there."

The week that followed was a busy one for Vince.

"I'm callin' Brooklyn, guys from my school, guys from my neighborhood. I'm callin' everybody, guys from 29th Street, and I'm tellin' them, 'Listen, we're gonna have a big fight up at the 'Y'."

Vince's hard work paid off. Most of the guys he called showed up at the YWCA dance the following weekend.

"My friends were all there, and these guys from up there, where Virginia lived, they came upstairs. The next thing you know the fight breaks out. The guys from my neighborhood and all the other neighborhoods they're doin' really good with fuckin' chains, fists and everything... This guy, Philly Pork Chops, he hit this guy from up there; beat the shit out of him. Guys that I was with were doin' good except for one thing—I wasn't fightin'. I was watchin' and I'm psyched. I'm goin', 'Yeah! Yeah! Yeah!'"

After the fight was over, Vince would learn a lesson from his friends that would last forever.

"They fuckin' cornered me, and I thought I was gonna die. They said, 'Ya cocksucker!' Ya skinny little motherfucker. Ya make us all come up here.' I was always a good salesman. 'You make us come up here ta fuckin' fight for ya and ya little cocksucker—ya don't even fight.' That was the last time I ever pulled that shit. I fought after that. Oh, yeah."

Going out with Virginia got Vince out of his neighborhood and up to 95th Street and First Avenue.

"Oh, this was a new neighborhood for me. I went up there. I was—like given the candy store. Ooh, this was a real tough guy neighborhood. See 51st Street never did it for me, somethin' was really missin' there. I wanted more. There wasn't enough excitement. I wanted more danger. There were some tough guys in my neighborhood, don't get me wrong. They dressed with the pompadour haircuts, the collar up and the pegged pants, the taps and everything.

"The guys I remember on 51st Street were Gaten Dario, (oh, he taught me a lot of shit) and Junior "JR", and there was Willy the Greek, Nicky the Greek, Franky the Frog. Franky was a Frenchmen so we called him Franky the Frog. There was a guy we called Alley Boy and then there was a gang, a motorcycle gang down the street that this guy Paulie belonged to. The Black Rebels Motorcycle Club they were called. I think it was the same name as the club that Marlon Brando had in *The Wild One*.

"JR was the first guy I got laid with. He fixed me up with this broad in the neighborhood, Irene Bianco. Irene usta be an opera singer, but she was fuckin', suckin' everybody's dick in the neighborhood. I usta hang with JR. JR was like my mentor. I usta wear my hair like his. Walk like him. I was 14. JR was already 20 or 21."

When Vince was 16, one of the guys on 51st Street saved him from making a fatal mistake. "Me and this kid, Vito, we went out to Sunnyside, Queens to see these two rich girls that we had met. We were walkin' down the street with the girls. These Irish guys, big guys, a whole bunch of them, they were standin' on the corner. We were little compared to these guys. Their leader was this guy they called Mikey the Bear. They made some remarks about guineas. I turned around to say somethin'. The girl grabbed my arm and said, 'Ignore them. Just keep walkin'.'

"We left, but our egos were tremendously bruised. Nobody can talk to us like that. We got in the car and on the way home we're thinkin' these fuckin' guys they can't get away with this. There's no way they're gonna get away with this. We were enraged.

"So we went up to Vito's house. He had a sawed off shotgun in his closet. We were goin' back there and I was gonna blow this guy away. So we got the shotgun and everything and we're gettin' inta the car to go back there. Gaten Dario saw us and he says, 'What are ya guys doin'?

He knew somethin' was up and then he saw the shotgun. He said, 'What the fuck ya doin' with this?'

"He grabbed me by the hair and pulled me out of the car. He smacked me. 'What are ya doin'?' So when we told him, he got all crazy. Really, he saved our lives 'cause I definitely was gonna shoot this guy. No two ways about it. I had it in my mind that I was blowin' this fuckin' guy away."

Today, Vince claims that was the first Godshot in his life. "I would'a probably wound up dead or in the electric chair."

"But eventually, JR and the guys on 51st Street disappeared out of my life. See, those guys weren't tough enough for me. Oh, no, I had to go where the real fuckin' tough guys were. When I really got to go where I knew where the money was and who to hang out with was when I got outta the joint.

**

School was always the furthest thing from Vince's mind as a youngster, but it would eventually be one of the ways that he would meet tougher guys than himself. "When I was in school, every year I had the worst marks. I was always in trouble. With my 'ADD' and not payin' attention, and wanting to hang out with the older tough guys. My head was up my ass."

Vince attended P.S. 135 elementary school which was right in his neighborhood. "I was a terrible student. I was really bad. My parents were in school more than I was. But it was my mother that was always there. My father never showed an interest in my schoolwork, or anythin' having to do with my schooling. You know Italians, they leave it up to the mother to take care of those kind of things."

Then Vince went to P.S. 59 Junior High School. "That's where I was starting to get inta hangin' out. Guys would ask, 'Where did ya hang out?' I was like, shit. I hung out all over.

And when I was in the 7th and 8th grade I started to drift towards hanging out in different neighborhoods where all the tough guys hung out. I hung out on 45th Street, on 55th Street. I broke away from 51st Street because 51st Street was not really happenin'. The guys I was friends with on 51st Street had become like squares, and I started hangin' out with these tougher guys. It was like I was still afraid. In fact, I don't think I had beat up that guy [Louie] yet. I was afraid but I was mesmerized with tough guys. I had a way about me that the toughest guys in whatever neighborhood I went inta sorta befriended me. I always made sure that the toughest guys in the neighborhoods I hung out not only protected me, but really liked me. In other words, I was testin' the waters already. At that time, my ambition was to be a juvenile delinquent."

There was obviously something missing in Vince's life that led him astray. "I was lookin' for love. I was lookin' for acceptance. I mean I didn't know that. But what I really wanted was people to look up to me instead of beatin' me up. Respect. It was like a sorta respect."

Despite his many problems in school, Vince had artistic abilities that could have easily turned his life around, and his school years could have been fruitful. He could draw and was given awards and prizes for his artwork. He also liked acting.

"Every year from the second grade all the way up to the eight-grade, they usta have a play, a major play in the school, and they always picked me to play the lead. And I was good, too. I played some really good parts."

It started when he played Jupiter. "I was the King of the Gods of all the planets. In Junior High, I remember one part—Saint Patrick. I found out Saint Patrick was an Italian, and they sent him to Ireland to kill the snakes. So, of course, when I started drinkin'—Saint Patty's Day was a great excuse to drink.

"Yeah, I liked acting, and I really was good at it. In fact, I usta look like Sal Mineo when I was a kid. "Madone," the girls I usta have. They were all crazy about Sal Mineo so I capitalized on his looks."

Vince's talent in art paid off on several occasions. "I usta belong to Kips Bay Boys Club, and I won a bicycle for paintin' somethin' on the wall." Even more impressive was the art scholarship he won to Music and Art High School. "I took a test when I was in eight grade for Music and Arts High School and I passed the test. Now Music and Art for me was like being a fish out of water. By that time, I already acquired the look of the pompadour, the pegged pants, and the silk shirts with the collar turned up in the back, and the featherweight shoes. Featherweights were real thin-soled shoes that turned up a little in the front. In other words, you couldn't even see the sole. It was paper thin, and we'd put taps on them. We had the leather jackets then, too." This was the style of dress tough street guys like Vince embraced in the 1950s.

"So when I went up to Music and Art on 137th Street, I got out of the subway and you gotta walk up all these steps to get to school. So I go up the steps, and I was a little scared, too, 'cause I didn't know what to expect. I walked up that last step and there was a long flat surface which led to the front doors. On that flat surface, there were all the guys and the girls in the whole school waitin' to get inta school. 'Cause we still had an hour to kill before school started, I walked over that step and everybody looked at me like who the f... Who is this guy?"

Vince stuck out like a sore thumb from these more affluent kids who wore chino pants with the buckle in the back. The Ivy League style as it was called was in at Music and Art. The boys wore button down shirts with white buck shoes, and crew haircuts. "I looked at them and they looked at me. Everybody was lookin'. And, then, I looked over to the right and I saw that there were about eight or nine guys that looked like me. I played it pretty sharp. I kept walkin' and stayed by myself. I figured, *We'll see what happens.*" Sure enough within a week, I was friends with these guys, Paulie Sorrento, Frankie Tominello. Frankie became a good friend of mine, and there were a few other guys, too. We were all Italian and we all knew how to draw. We were great artists. But faget about it, we were like outcasts. Well, of course, all the girls liked us, and all the Jewish girls were crazy about us, too."

But being a student at Music and Art compounded Vince's feelings of inadequacy and led to trouble. The guys he hung around with were as bad as he was. After one year Vince and all his friends were expelled. "They said, 'You gotta go.' We just didn't fit in. They knew it."

From there, they sent him to the High School of Commerce on the West Side. "And when I went there, I got involved with these Italian guys which were in a gang called the Harlem Red Wings. In fact, most of those guys that were in the Red Wings wound up in the Gambino Crime Family or the Genovese Crime Family when they got older. The Red Wings were a steppingstone. They went from the Red Wings to organized crime."

The Harlem Red Wings were among the most notorious teen gangs in the city. In addition to going to school with some of its members, he also became good friends with another Red Wing that he worked with at Gristedes Supermarket on 55th Street. "He was a delivery boy. He invited me to a dance and he said, 'I'm with the Harlem Red Wings.' And I said, *'Whow!'* I mean they had a reputation. And he says to me, 'Why don't ya come up ta the dance?'

"So I go up to the dance. I got in tight with these guys and then I started goin' out with one of the girls from Harlem. They saw I was a little nuts and they asked me to jump in with them. I hung out in Harlem, 107th and Pleasant. We usta go to all the dances up there. These guys were tough bastards, a tough fuckin' gang. Once you were in with them, you got that red jacket with the fuckin' red wings on the back. Oh, it was beautiful. It's like you arrived.

"Those were the days when the Italians and the Puerto Ricans and blacks were all fightin' each other. We were fightin' the Commanche Dragons, a Puerto Rican gang from Harlem. We were fightin' the Sportsmans and the MauMau Chaplins out of Brooklyn. They usta call them gang fighters and all those gangs—jitter bugging. Whereas today, they call them gang bangers and gang bangin'.

"I usta always carry long Italian switch blades with the buttons, the ones where the blade comes out the side. Stilettos, where you push the button, it jumped outta your hand. I usta sit in front of the mirror practicing with this switch blade for hours. Oh, I was mental, a little psychotic, too. I wanted to achieve somethin'. Some kids wanna grow up to be a doctor. I wanted to grow up to be a hoodlum!

"I was waiting for the opportunity that some day I was gonna 'shank' somebody. I had a guy in my neighborhood that showed me how to use a knife; a lot of guys were good with knives back then. He showed me how to come up and under; switch it from hand to hand."

Vince was in a few gang fights but he had never gotten to use his skills with a knife until one night. "We were fightin' the Commanche Dragons on the staircase in school and this Puerto Rican came at me. I pulled out the stiletto and he pulled out this Mickey Mouse switchblade. He was tryin' to stick me in the throat, and he went under my chin and cut me; all the nerves in my chin came out. He gave me a scar under my chin. I cut him, too, and they put me in the principal's office for that—the cops came. I started a 'rap'— what they call a 'juvy sheet.'"

Despite being put on record as a confirmed juvenile delinquent, something he was really proud of, Vince got away with the incident. His parents were called to school, and he felt betrayed by them. They said, "We don't know why he's like this. We come from good stock. He's incorrigible. We can't do anything with him."

"It was like right away—I was guilty before proven innocent. You know, total disloyalty. Not even asking, 'Did he do it?' But I had done what I did.

"I got in a couple of more fights after that, and believe it or not, I went and took another art's scholarship course at Industrial Arts. I lasted there until graduation. The only thing, I had an English teacher that usta call me, 'Ceeassy.' And I remember one day saying to her, 'Ya know for an English teacher your not too smart that ya can't pronounce my name.' She failed me and I couldn't graduate."

That summer brought more trouble Vince's way. "I got arrested when we mugged some fags in Central Park. We'd go up to the park and there was a certain section where they hung out. We'd walk over there and we'd mug them. Take their watches and everything. I felt bad about that 'cause I was always the type of guy—I never liked to hurt people that couldn't defend themselves. I didn't give a fuck if I could go after the kind of guy that deserved it, or a big guy who was givin' me a good fight. But this... It was to get money and we were drunk, but it wasn't right.

"We were so stupid that we were just goin' from one bunch of guys to another to another to another, not realizin' that they were runnin' for the police. We figured, *Ah, they ain't gonna say nothin', fuck it.* It was like a game. And sure enough, we're runnin' up a hill and there's cops here, cops there, cops everywhere, and they grabbed us. They arrested me. That got me another count on my juvy sheet, but I got away with that one, too."

From shoplifting at 13, and all through his teens, to pulling his first armed robbery was an easy transition for Vince. As a member of the Red Wings, guns were easily obtainable. At 18, Vince got arrested for an armed robbery.

"It was a stick up of a store. It was like a grocery type store. They sold coffee there and everything. It was a

Mickey Mouse score. I went in there with a gun. They actually slapped me on the wrist for that one."

But Vince's luck wouldn't last much longer. "I pulled another armed robbery with two of the guys from the Red Wings. It was a jewelry store that we hit. A cop came along during the robbery and pulled a gun out. I went for the gun I had in my bag, but he froze me out. I dropped my gun. I got arrested for that and the other guys got away with it because I kept my mouth shut. I did three years, and when I came out, they treated me like I was a king.

"They sent me to Elmira Reformatory and then from Elmira Reformatory I went to West Coxsackie. They took all the guys that liked to fight a lot and put them in Coxsackie 'cause they called that 'Gunfight at the OK Corral'."

CHAPTER 4

The Ringman Years

After Vince's beating at the mercy of the Coxsackie guards, he laid naked on the cold cement floor in a pool of his own blood. The next morning, the guards picked him up and took him to the infirmary. He was beaten pretty badly. But despite his tough guy demeanor, he was glad he wasn't dead.

"At the infirmary, the guards pretend that you fell, you hurt yourself, whatever. 'Cause it's all a crew. Up there, you're at their mercy. They're legal gangsters. So after three years of that, you're not workin' with a full deck."

After all the fights and time spent in the hole, Vince had pushed the limit with the guards and put his life in jeopardy. "I'm like Johnny Ringo up there–the guy in the old western movies. I got a rep as a badass, fuckin' guy. Meanwhile, I was scared to death inside, but I never let them know it. So the wire came down, they were ready to release me from the 'hole.' A guy comes up and he says, 'They're gonna put ya in the kitchen and Ringman is lookin' ta straighten ya out, or else.'"

Vince knew what "or else" meant and he knew about Ringman. He was the sadistic guard that ran the kitchen.

"Ringman's nickname was Meat Face. He had eight people with him in the kitchen that were brutal sadists like him. I couldn't get a job on the outside, like the piggery, the dairy or somethin' else. You had to earn that. Don't get me wrong, there were bad people in the piggery, and in the dairy, but they were smart. They weren't in trouble all the time like me. They wouldn't put me in a shop, either, 'cause they didn't trust me. So I wound up in the kitchen. When you're a fuck up, you go to the kitchen. The kitchen cooked for over 700 men."

Ringman was certain Vince would fuck up again. It was rumored throughout the institution that if you fucked up in Ringman's kitchen and were taken into his office you were never seen again.

"And my motto was live fast, die young, make a beautiful corpse. So it was almost exciting to think that I was important enough that they wanted to whack me. So I went down in the kitchen, but I was smart then. This is the time where I used my brains and not my fuckin' stupidity. Inside of me, I knew I wasn't a bad person. There was always this push-pull thing goin' on in me. I knew I was tough, physically tough, and on the outside I looked tough, but inside I knew I wasn't tough at all.

"Now Ringman has this all set for me. He says to me [speaks in gruff voice], 'Aah, so ya been in the fuckin' hole. Ya know, ya think ya got it made in this place. Well your in the kitchen now and things are gonna change.'

Acting like a wise guy, I said, "Okay.'

"Well ya know everyday we cook here and at night the pots and pans have to all be washed and scrubbed. I'm gonna show ya what ya gotta do."

"He takes me over to these fuckin' pots and pans that the afternoon crew didn't do 'cause he had that job lined up for me. Usually it's two, three people that do it. But he says, 'I'm gonna let ya do this by yourself.' I swear to God, I never seen so many fuckin' pots and pans in my life. Pots that you can hide in that's how big they were, cauldrons and oars and spoons that the kitchen used. We're talkin' about ladles that weighed more than I did.

"I said to him, 'all right I'll do it.' After seein' that pile, I wasn't actin' like no asshole, no tough guy.'

"I'm gonna come back here in a couple of hours ta see how ya did. I expect to see this place immaculate, shinin'. I don't wanna see one bit of grease anywhere."

"I knew how to clean. So I said to myself, *Fuck! I can do this*. Oh, but I hated it. I mean I was dyin' inside. But, I thought, *Fuck. I gotta protect myself here*. I knew what he was up to. So I started washin'. My fingers were raw to the bone from the Brillo, and I'm scrubbin' and scrubbin'. Finally, after three hours, I'm half dead. He comes in expectin' to see me fucked up or expectin' me to say, 'Fuck you. Stick your pots and pans up your ass.' And he would'a had the perfect excuse to take me in the office.

"He looks at the pots and pans. I'll never forget that look. He had a scowl on his face all the time, but his eyes lit up. He couldn't believe what he saw. And I did it all by myself in three, four hours. Even though he knew I did a perfect job, he took his hand. He had a white glove on. He went from one end of the sink to the other and he looked at the glove and it was clean. So I got through that night. He didn't really know what to say. He finally said, 'Hah! All right, that's good! All right, well tomorrow ya got the same job.' Well I did this forever."

Working in the kitchen wasn't Vince's only responsibility. "In the morning I had hall detail. We're talkin' about a joint that's about forty times—maybe a hundred times the size of a normal house and you have to mop the floors. They had a certain way of doin' it. One guy went down with the long cloth broom that catches the dirt. Then, you got guys behind with soapy mops, then, you got clear water, and dry mops. So, they had me doin' that in the morning, and in the afternoon, I was back in the kitchen washin' pots and pans."

Vince had been doing his assignments for some time without getting himself on the wrong side of Ringman or the other guards in the kitchen. "You'd work eight, nine hours a day. The morning thing was three, four hours. Then they had me in the kitchen 'til nighttime. So he comes up to me, 'cause he was pleased with what I did, but he wouldn't show it. I was a fuck-up. That's what he thought. Well there was this steam table that's probably about 20-feet long. They steam things on it. Underneath the steam table there's all these valves and pipes that look like a person's intestines— all twisted and everything. These pipes are copper and all green with mold. And he says to me, 'Ciacci, see those pipes and valves under there?'"

"Yeah."

"Those pipes and valves are fuckin' filthy. I want ya to make 'em shine. Do ya know what a piece of new copper looks like?"

"Sorta."

"Holdin' up a piece of copper pipe, he says, 'Ya see this? This is a new piece of copper. I wanna see ya make those pipes look like this."

"I got a little scared then. 'Cause I said to myself, *This motherfucker... Are ya fuckin' crazy?* To do one pipe would take you a whole day. Well I did it. I was cryin' inside. My fingers were all raw. You'd get splinters—I had pieces of fuckin' steel wool in my fingers. I was doin' this thing, and I had blood all over my hands, but I kept doin' it and doin' it. I don't know how long it took me, a week, two weeks, but I did it.

"Now, this is where things started to change. My life could'a changed forever if I would'a had the mentality I had when I was doin' does pots and pans, and when I was doin' that thing under the steam table."

But Vince being Vince with ambitions to be a tough guy would only change his ways while in Ringman's kitchen. After a while, Ringman saw through Vince's tough guy deamor and Vince's life was no longer in danger.

"I got accepted when he saw how clean those pipes were. He looked at me with respect." Vince thought to himself, *Fuck you! I'm not gonna fuck-up like I did before*, and I did it. I thought I saw tears in his eyes.

"Ringman with laughter in his voice said, 'Ah, look at those fuckin' pipes. Ya sure ya did 'em by yourself?'

"I said, 'Who the hell's gonna help me do this?' I felt a little more relaxed with him."

"Ah, ya did a great job."

Nevertheless, Vince got a little worried the next day when Ringman called him into his office, and said, "Ya know what? No more pots and pans for you. I'm gonna put ya on 'extra.'"

Extra meant Vince would be doing a lot of different types of jobs in the kitchen. "Anythin' they need you for they put you on. One day you're workin' with the cooks, one day you're workin' around the sinks, one day you're helpin' the guy in the icebox. It was hard work but it was nothin' next to what I had been doin'. So I'm extra for a month. Ringman looked at me differently now. He even started to talk to me different, and the guards were talkin' to me different.

"I was goin' out in the yard during the day to the back wall. Rumors were goin' around about me workin' for Ringman. They would say, 'That fuckin' Ringman hasn't killed ya yet? Your alive. Your still alive. Aah, look he's still here.' They usta break my balls. They knew about the pots and the pans, which gave me credibility with my crew, 'cause they knew for a skinny little fuck I could take care of myself in any situation."

After a short time, things would change again for Vince when the first cook's sentence was over and he went home. "The cooks are: first cook, second cook, third cook. The third cook's got the shitiest job. The first cook is like the king. Second cook's got it easy. He helps cook and prepares dinner for the institution. So Ringman says to me, 'I'm gonna put ya on the cooks.'

"Which I said to myself, *Wow, this is an honor*. Little did I realize that when they cook, they got those big vents goin' all around the whole fuckin' kitchen and there's grease in those vents. Well the third cook's fuckin' job is to crawl in there and clean the grease. On Sunday's, we'd do the vents. I had a few extras on there with me, too. You talk about a greased pig. You come out of there at the end of the day and you're fuckin' filthy, but it wasn't like a punishment. I was becomin' a cook. I also helped with other things in the kitchen."

By that time, Vince's sentence was drawing closer to the end. He wasn't getting in trouble anymore and Ringman had gained more and more confidence in him.

"All of sudden, the first cook who was a Good Boy got in a fight. If you get in a fight you lose your privileges in the kitchen, unless you're a fuck-up and you were on the pots and pans already. You do your five day strippo, then you do your assign, then you come right back to the pots and pans. You can't go lower than that. But, if you got a good position like a cook, first cook—you got it made. You can eat whatever you want. They treat you like royalty. So he got in a fight and lost the first cook position, and I became second cook. Second cook became first cook, and they put a guy from extras on as third cook. So now I'm second cook, Ringman's startin' to talk to me like I'm one of his own. He started callin' me Nicky. He started callin' me Ciacci in a nice tone of voice. I remember once he said, 'Nicky, come here. Whatta ya think about this?'

"It was somethin' to do with the cookin', the oars, or somethin'. I thought, *He's askin' me what I think.* I told him what I thought, but you know I started to feel important for once in my life.

"Then after a few more months as second cook, the first cook went home 'cause his time was up. So, Ringman calls me inta 'is office. He says, 'Well, ya got a year left in this joint. Your doin' really good. Your not gettin' in anymore fights.' I didn't have to get in anymore fights. There were guys in my crew that loved me, and said, 'If anybody fucks with ya, we'll take care of 'em 'cause we're with ya. They get killed. And Johnny Goomba took me under his wing."

But Johnny's friendship would prove detrimental for Vince in the long run. "So, I'm first cook now, and I'm fuckin' flyin'. I cooked the meals. We usta cook in these three broilers. There were oars. Can you image cookin' with oars? Baked beans in vats. We're talkin' about enough baked beans to last you five years. I'm cookin' them for one dinner, along with franks. We'd make chicken and pork chops. I'm barkin' orders at other people. Believe it or not, I was runnin' the kitchen. Me! Ringman and this little old man that died while I was there. We cried when he died.

"He was the civilian cook, a real professional cook. Or, maybe you should call him a dietician. He saw that we got the right vitamins, or whatever. I loved that little old man. He was a delicate little guy, such a nice guy. He must have been in his sixties, seventies with just a little white hair on his head. Oh, he was crazy about me; he loved me that guy. He usta put his arm around me all the time. He was terrific that guy.

"When I met that little old man, it was like I experienced his sense of decency. He treated me like a human being. I had the respect I always wanted. One day, he got a heart attack and died. He was like the father I always wanted. He usta talk to me and tell me, 'Ya know you'll get outta this place. This time, you have a chance.'"

All the praise and good sentiment Vince was receiving was beginning to have a positive affect. "You know I was actually listenin' to these guys. I actually had it in my mind that I wanted to straighten out my life. 'Cause up to then I wasn't doin' too good."

With six months left on his sentence Vince was eligible for a parole board hearing. "Nobody goes to the parole board with six months left. They go to the parole board with two years left and they get paroled. When I got out, I saw a lot of guys on the street that I started doin' business with that were smarter than me. They didn't get inta fights and got paroled.

The worst of the worst got paroled and these guys were bad news. They should'a never got paroled.

"So I go before the parole board, and they said, 'This is just a formality for you because you're not getting a parole."

"I know that."

"You've been a real fuck-up up until now and all of a sudden you've changed your ways. All right, so we're not giving you parole because you didn't deserve it for all the stuff you've done up until you were in the kitchen. But we're hoping that when you leave here what you learned in the kitchen and the way you've been treating yourself for the last year that you're gonna take these skills and values with you.'

"I felt like tellin' them to go shove it. Well that was the tough guy in me. I had friends that usta tell the parole board, 'I got fifteen months left. I'll do it on my fuckin' head. Go fuck yourself!' They'd throw them in the hole."

But Vince was starting to wise up and kept his mouth shut. "I was still thinkin' about Ringman killin' me. So I went back that night and I was a little depressed 'cause Virginia, my girlfriend, was ready to leave me. I got a Dear John letter from her. It broke my heart. She was my first love. In fact, I still got the tattoo on my arm with her name.

"That night, Ringman knew I wasn't feelin' right and calls me in his office. He talked to me like a father. He says, 'Ya know Ciacci. In a way, I'm glad that they didn't parole ya. I knew ya were gonna get your max. But you're gonna be here in the kitchen for six more months. Your're a skinny little fuck. I'm gonna fatten ya up. I'm takin' ya off the kitchen and givin' ya the icebox.'"

This was yet another promotion for someone that came to the kitchen as a marked man.

"Well you know how much work you do in the icebox? There's three iceboxes, one with milk, one with all the food that was eaten during the day, pork chops, steaks. When you got the icebox, you can eat anythin' you want. You can throw a steak on the fuckin' grill anytime. At night, you load up the cart and you bring food to the guys in solitary. 'Cause they gotta eat, too. I'd cook for the officers. Sometimes dignitaries would come in you'd cook for them. And whatever I cooked I could eat. Nobody else in the kitchen could eat like that. They catch you eatin' in the kitchen, you're dead. You go in the hole. Me—I could eat in front of the guards in front of anybody. So I had the icebox with the puddin's, and all the milk. I'd make milkshakes or some eggs. Man, I had it made. I'm eatin' and eatin' but there was somethin' about my metabolism that I couldn't get fat. I'm doin' fifteen minutes of work in the afternoon; an hour's worth of work at night with the carts, and I'd enjoy that 'cause I'd go up to solitary."

Everybody was treating Vince differently. The guards in solitary that had previously been beating him up had a new respect for him. Ringman was his buddy and giving him fatherly advice. When he was in the yard, the Good Boys treated him with respect and watched out for him.

"In the yard, I'm considered what they call a 'gee.' A gee is a guy commands respect. That's a gunfighter to the max that's made it. It's like you're 'makin' your bones' in the joint. You don't 'whack' nobody, but you're made, you're set. Nobody can touch you. Which deep inside, I knew I wasn't a gee. But they thought I was. And, you know, I had to watch out for the blacks that were lookin' for a rep that would come after me, but I had protection, like a shield around me."

The Good Boys were Vince's protection and his ticket to a new life when he got out of Coxsackie.

"My problems really began when I got out of the joint. If I would'a been smart, listened to Ringman tellin' me about how great I was, and that I changed, and that he'd never seen anybody change like me. He was always givin' me advice and love. If I would'a done what they told me when I was a cook, 'Go out there get a job as a cook. You could work in

49

any restaurant. We'll give you a certificate.' But no, I'd go in the yard and listen to Johnny Goomba. He grabs me and says, 'Ya know I got two years left to my max. You're gettin' out in another couple of months. Ya wanna make some money? I wanna hook ya up with my father and some guys who ya can make your bones.' And I wasn't that involved with mob guys in those days. I was like a gangbanger. I knew nothin' about the mob."

But back out on the streets Vince would receive a new education and have ambitions of being a made-man (a member of Mafia's inner circle) in the New York Mafia.

CHAPTER 5

Gettin' Out and Gettin' Wings

Vince was 21 years old in 1962 when he was released from Coxsackie. John F. Kennedy was President and Frank Sinatra's "Rat Pack" were the coolest guys around. It's difficult to say whether guys in the mob modeled themselves after the Rat Pack or vice-versa. Both wore snappy clothes and had lifestyles the average working man could hardly imagine. This was the lifestyle Vince immediately fell into.

"I'm goin' from dressin' in the tight pants and the kind of clothes I usta wear to wearin' silk suits, mohair suits, fuckin' Italian knits, diamond rings and alligator shoes."

But Vince's life would take a turn that most mob guys at the time would never follow.

"A lot of the Red Wings—their fathers were big shots in the mob. The word got out that I was a 'stand up guy.' So when I got out of the joint, my friends called me up to Harlem. They wanted me to stay with my crew so I was on my way. I had a ticket to ride. But it was in the wrong direction. I should have listened to Ringman.

"So, I go up to Harlem. It was like Napoleon returning from Elba. I went in the neighborhood, and girls knew who I was. I fucked the most beautiful broad the day I got out because of the guys. The Harlem guys said, 'Hey, this fuckin' guy never opened up his fuckin' mouth. What a fuckin' guy.' But it was a feelin' that killed me. 'Cause in my head I thought, *If they only knew*. If they ever found out who I really was. I still felt like I wasn't good enough."

Jo Jo Argenteri who was Capo at the time of the Harlem Genovese Crew was into heroin smugglin'. Jo Jo got hold of Vince and said, "We got the word that you were up in

Coxsackie. We heard un-fuckin' believable stories. You're a wild guy, man. We wanna take care of ya.'

"So they opened up a satchel with money and they dumped it on me. 'This is your's. We're sendin' ya ta the Fountainebleu and everythin's paid for. Down there ya look up certain people in Miami Beach.'

"I didn't know how to act with all this acceptance. Anyway, I took the money and the vacation."

Vince still hadn't followed up on Johnny Goomba's referral. "When I came back from Florida, I went down to Brooklyn to meet Johnny's people. Next thing you know, I'm gettin' set up with armed robberies.

"I'm still living at home, and my father and mother don't know what the fuck is goin' on, but they knew I was up to no good. When they usta come up and see me, one part of them felt guilty, the other part—they wanted to call me every name in the book. When I got out, I found out my mother threw out all the pictures of me, my comic books, my picture cards. That's how old Italians were. And when I got out, they mistrusted me. "

With Vince's new acceptance he found he had many new friends all over the city. Through Johnny Goomba he was working with guys in Brooklyn. "Then I met these guys from Little Italy. I was confused about where to stay. I'm goin' to Harlem, goin' to the Bronx, goin' to Brooklyn. I'm like a piece of shit. I'm all over. And I'm makin' money here. I'm makin' money there. I'm doin' armed robberies. We did a little 'shylockin.' Then I worked for guys 'breakin legs.' We did it all."

Vince also kept in touch with his other friends from Coxsackie who were now out on the street. But as street smart as he was, he didn't know about his friend's drug use. "I'm hangin' out with Billy Grasso in Corona [Queens]. Billy was one of my friends in the joint. Billy is the other side of the coin from Johnny Goomba. Billy's a 'junkie.'"

At the time, Vince was both naïve about drugs, and that Billy was a heroin addict. "I'm hangin' with Billy and Mastretti—Tony Mas they usta to call him which was Johnny Goomba's right hand man. But Johnny Goomba didn't know that Mastretti was 'shootin' dope.' So, I'm with Billy Grasso, Johnny Mas, Solly the Jew, another guy that did time with us, he was a junkie, too.

"So here I am caught between a rock and a hard place. I loved Billy, and I remember one night we go up to Harlem, and I see Billy—he's doin' somethin' with his hands with this black guy, and he jumps back in his convertible. See we usta go from across the Triboro Bridge inta Harlem. I didn't know nothin' about drugs... heroin, not anythin', and I said to Billy, 'What the hell are ya doin' out there?'"

"Ah, I got a scam in with these black guys."

"Whatta ya fuckin' with moulinyans for?"

"He kept doin' this over the next few weeks, and I didn't understand what he was doin'. Then one day we're in his house. Billy's in the bathroom. I said, 'Billy, come on! Whatta ya doin'? Come on let's go out!'

"He answers in a groggy voice, 'Ah... Oh, I'll be right... I'll be right there. Ah...'"

"What the fuck are ya doin'? Come on out!"

"Fifteen minutes go by and he was still in there so I kicked the bathroom door in. There's Billy with a 'spike' in his arm. He was 'on the nod.' To see my good friend with a needle in his arm, 'noddin' out,' it broke my heart. I ran over, grabbed the spike out of his arm, and I started beatin' the shit outta him. Blood all over the place... I went crazy. But he had a way of talkin' that I didn't run away from him. There was somethin' that kept me there."

Vince continued to hang around with Billy. "But I'm not doin' any drugs. All I'm doin' is drinkin'. I'm like a chameleon. I'm goin' to Johnny Goomba's neighborhood. And I'm goin' out with this girl from the sixth ward down in Little Italy—Lillian LaVauchie.

It was either his dysfunctional relationship with Lillian or inevitable that Vince's life would change forever. "There was one night me and Lillian had a big fight and I was drinkin'. I was so depressed. Lillian and me we had such a torrid affair. I was cheatin' on her, and she was gorgeous. It's funny I always had the best lookin' girls when I was real young. They were attracted to my insanity and I wasn't a bad lookin' guy. I had the most beautiful girls in the sixth ward, and they were always trouble. So, Lillian and me were breakin' up and I'm heartbroken. We're at Billy's house. Now, all these guys were there, Solly the Jew, Mastretti, this guy Little Red, and Billy. They all had all these 'cookers' on the table. In those days, I didn't know what the fuck they were doin'. They had this look in their eye, and they're 'cookin' this shit up, and the next thing you know Mas 'shot up,' and I said, 'What the fuck are ya all doin', man?'

"I remember takin' the spike off the table. There was about fifty dollars worth of heroin—which was cheap then. The last thing I said was, 'If ya don't give me some of this, I'm throwin' this away.'

"Of course, if I threw it away, they would'a killed me, friend or no friend. I realized that later when I started usin' heroin. Billy 'skin-popped' me, and there was no more sufferin'. I forgot all about me and Lillian. It was beautiful. It wasn't even a vein. It was just a shot under the skin.' We call that 'gettin' your wings.' And it was just like that.

"After that I was a junkie, too, but I was a smart junkie. Or at least that's what I thought. When I would get my dope, I would usually be with Billy and Mas, and by the way, if Johnny Goomba knew about the dope, I would'a been dead, and he would'a killed Mas first."

CHAPTER 6

Saborito and Me

Life had change drastically for Vince since he was back on the street. Now along with his alcohol usage, he was also a heroin user and he was in tight with "the boys."

"I had my eyes set on 'gettin' made'. And I gotta tell ya somethin', I was the best dresser in the neighborhood. 'Cause when I usta see a 'wise guy,' a 'made guy' or a 'capo' with somethin' special, I'd go and buy it. I was fanatical, and addicted to fuckin' clothes. I mean you should see the clothes I wore. But no car! There was somethin' about me and cars that I didn't wanna fuck with. 'Cause I drank, and I knew that if I drank, I couldn't drive and besides that why'd I have to drive when everybody I was with had cars. These guys I hung out with, Johnny Goomba's crew—they all had Cadillacs, fuckin' Mercedes. Oh, we also took cabs, and once in a while, we even got limos.

"When I came outta the joint, I started to go to night clubs, too. One night I go to a club on 45th Street with a few guys from downtown, and who's the bouncer, Jimmy Saborito. Jimmy and I were 'very tight' upstate. Jimmy was on the Good Boy wall, but he was like a bull this guy. Madone was he a tough bastard. He was like one of these football players. They hit you and you're dead. He wasn't that intelligent, but he loved me this guy. We had a good little rapport. I hadn't seen Jimmy in a long time. Jimmy went home before me, and I called him when I got out. I didn't get the right number or somethin'. Then I ran inta him at this club. We loved each other.

"We started goin' to the beach during the day. We were tryin' to figure out what to do. So I came up with this brainstorm and said to him, 'We can get some guns. At night, we go to Cherry Hill, New Jersey or Jamaica Estates in Queens and we do armed robberies."

Vince would use his acting skills, wear a disguise, knock on the door, pull a gun walk right in and rob the house. "I usta use a Puerto Rican accent. Call Jimmy a Puerto Rican name. He'd call me a Puerto Rican name. We were masked, and we'd say things to make people think, oh these are armed robbers from New Jersey. We knew what we were doin'.

"So we kept doin' this for a long time. The message here is: if there is a God, I should be dead. We always made sure that people knew we weren't gonna hurt them, and nobody ever got hurt. We'd tie them up, tape them. After that we'd take what we wanted. Never hurt no women, nothin', no matter what they looked like, no fuckin' around."

The flaw in their plan was that they never 'cased' the houses they would rob. "We were a little stupid. We would look at a house and say, 'Oh, that's a good one.'

"One night, we did this place in Jamaica Estates. So we go in there 'on the blind.' I was so young I still had a baby face. I parted my hair and wore glasses with black rims, and a shirt with a college letter. I knocked on the door and a lady opened the door. I looked so innocent to her until I pulled my gun. I told her, 'Take it easy. Raise your hands.' Saborito came out of the shadows and we went in. So I'm tyin' her up downstairs, and Saborito is upstairs and he goes, 'Holy fuckin' shit!'

"I run upstairs and walk inta this bedroom, and there were hundreds of rifles, and handguns, and ammunition and knives. We're lookin' at these fuckin' guns with scopes and stuff. We run back downstairs, and say, 'What is this?'

"She goes, 'Well my husband is a cop. He's a gun collector.'

"And I'm thinkin', *Motherfucker! If this guy would'a been home.* We got these two Mickey Mouse fuckin' guns. I had a thirty-two and Sab had a twenty-five, and this fuckin' guy's got Magnums and fuckin' cannons upstairs."

The danger didn't occur to them until after they left the house. "I'm tellin' Saborito, 'this motherfucker's a cop and a marksman. If he would'a been in the house, ya know what would have happened to us?'

"We asked the woman, 'When's your husband comin' home?' She didn't want to tell us at first so we scared her a little and she said he was away."

"I said to myself, *If he comes back, we get shot.*"

"We took all the shit, all the guns, we put them in sheets. We had a truck and we loaded it up. We didn't even think anything else about it. That's how crazy we were. Nothin' stopped us. Then we go downtown that's where we really get fucked. 'Cause we were with the wise guys, right. We sold them over two-hundred thousand worth of guns. They gave us, for the whole fuckin' lot, twenty-grand.

"I should be gone today, I was so fuckin' reckless. That's how we lived. It got to the point Saborito had to get rid of me. He had a girlfriend. My friends that had girlfriends hated me because all I wanted to do is steal. I had a lot of girlfriends, but I was only interested in stealin'. At least, some of these guys wanted to be in love. So Saborito one day says to me, 'Ya know. Ya may know what your talkin' about or maybe ya don't. Ya got this real snippy attitude about ya. I listen ta ya, but I'm gonna tell ya somethin' right now, it's over between us. No more. I can't do this shit no more. I'm in love with my girl. I wanna be with her and this ain't workin' no more.'

"Of course, I tried to con him inta stayin' with me.

"'It's over,' he said, 'Now, let's not make a big deal out of it.'

"Which meant if I continued he's gonna knock me on my ass. I backed off and that was the end of our partnership.

But we had a wonderful thing goin'. We musta pulled about 30 fuckin' armed robberies. And where'd all that money go? Drugs! Booze! Broads! What do they say... 'it burns a hole in your pocket.'"

CHAPTER 7

The Girls

Many of the girls Vince and his friends hung around with were the daughters of mob bosses or mob associates. So it's safe to say they didn't take shit from anyone, especially from Vince and his friends.

"Those were the days when girls usta wear teased hair. I usta go out with this girl, Niki, she was five-feet three and her hairdo was three-feet five. She had what they usta call the 'Page Boy Flip.' They were hysterical these girls. They were always chewin' gum—and tough. I mean you wanna see tough little fuckin' girls. They were it.

"I usta go down to Prince Street. I was hangin' out with this little guy who was a safe cracker. He was a real classy guy. This girl in the neighborhood loved me. She was a beautiful little blonde. Oh, she thought I was it. See if you don't know certain neighborhoods, if you go down there, and the girls see a new guy, whew, they go nuts. 'Cause they're usta the neighborhood guys."

At first Vince didn't know that this girl liked him or anything about her, but he began to figure it out real fast. He also didn't know that going out with her would not be healthy for him.

"Ah, she was hot, and every time I'd walk by she'd make suggestive remarks. Oh, God I wanted this girl so fuckin' bad. In those days, you'd go out with a girl, you'd fuck them and that was it."

This wasn't going to happen, as Vince would soon find out because she had a brother named Marco who had a nasty reputation and he was going to watch out for his sister's better interests.

"Marco hit a moulinyan once and split his head open like a grapefruit. He was one of those feared fuckin' guys. I knew him by reputation and to say hello and stuff. My friend told me, 'Ya know she likes ya, but ya betta watch out she's Marco's sister.'

"Well one night we're in this bar and Marco comes up to me—he says, 'Nicky, ya know, I hear nice things about ya. You're a good lookin' kid. Ya know what? I betcha a lotta girls like ya.'

"Just the way he looked at me, I was scared. 'Cause this motherfucker was twice my size. I liked my face, and I knew if he hit me in the face I'd have no face left. 'So I said, 'I do all right.'

"Look, my sister, she's a kid ya know, but she's got this crush on ya. Ya know the way kids are—these girls. They like this guy, that guy. Ya know what? Don't pay any attention ta her. Pretend she ain't got no crush on ya. Awright?'

"He put his hand on my forearm and squeezed it just enough and said, 'Awright, Nicky? I know ya know what I'm sayin'.'

"I thought I was gonna shit in my pants. And I said, 'Marco, I don't even look at her.'

"And I didn't—I wouldn't look at her anymore. If she was around, I pretended she didn't exist, and the word got out that I wouldn't go near her, and after a while she gave up on me.

"Oh Madone, this guy was scary. He was with 'the guys' when he got older and he eventually got his 'button' (he was a made-man). One night, they found him down on Prince Street in the middle of the street with three bullets in the back of his head. Wise guys might have done it. You don't want wise guys to be scared of you, and they were scared of him. Those are the guys that they nail first."

***

Vince's mother was either jealous of her son's girlfriends or overly protective. She told him that any girl that performed fellatio on Vince had done it to other guys and would even do it to other guys behind his back. This would haunt Vince for years and make him extremely jealous and mistrusting of the women in his life. Whenever, he brought a girl home to meet his parents, his mother would take the girl on the side and say, "Do you know he was in jail? Do you know he steals? Do you know he carries a knife and a gun?"

Is it any wonder that Vince would marry three times? His marriages like the rest of his life would be extremely passionate and mostly turbulent. "Denise was the first, and I met her at the Headliner. The wise guys from Little Italy, and the wise guys from Harlem owned the Headliner, a nightclub on 43rd Street and Eight Avenue.

"Denise walked inta the Headliner one night—she looked like Elizabeth Taylor. She was a beauty. So I hit on her right away. We danced and the next thing ya know we're havin' a good time. So after that I started goin' out with her. The guys from the neighborhood downtown, this guy Tommy Barboni goes out with her sister, and then my other friend Joey goes out with one of her friends. Denise' father was a bookmaker. They lived in New Brunswick, but the old man was doin' action in Newark."

Denise had already been married and had a little girl. The short-lived marriage ended in divorce. Vince found out about the ex-husband but had never met him.

"He was from New Jersey, too, Ronny Cannella. He found out about me, and there was a jealousy thing goin' on between us. We just developed this instant 'hard-on' for each other. He knew I was dating his ex-wife, and I knew I wanted to kill this prick because he had fucked my girl and I loved her."

Vince and Ronny wouldn't always feel this way about each other, and Ronny would be the one responsible for Vince almost seeing an early grave.

"So, we were like two gunfighters that were destined to meet. I wanted to get this prick. I was hopin' that he'd come down to the Headliner some night. So one rainy night we're drivin' around Manhattan in Denise's white, '64, Chevy Impala. She's drivin'. I'm in the passenger seat and her sister and girl friend are in the back seat. We're drivin' down Broadway and all of a sudden a Cadillac pulls alongside us. It's this guy Ronny with this other guy, big motherfucker named Fats, and four guys from Newark."

This would be Vince's first encounter with Fats and not the only time Fats would pose a threat to Vince's good looks. "Ronny knew it was me. He looked over and yells, 'Hey, Nicky! Nicky, ya prick! You're Nicky, hah?'

"I looked at him, and I said, 'That's right. Where ya goin'? Ya wanna come over and see me?'

"He didn't know it but I had a fuckin' gun under my shoulder. They jump outta the car. The streets were all shiny from the rain. It was a little eerie to tell you the truth. I jump outta the car with the gun in my hand, and I shove it in Ronny's fuckin' face. He almost fainted, and I said, 'What are ya gonna do now? See, this is the right odds. I got fuckin' nine in the clip and there's five of ya. So, we'll work it out. One apiece, two apiece.'

"I kept it in his face and said, 'Ya cocksucker. I'm goin' with your wife now. If ya want trouble, get ya whole fuckin' crew from Newark and come down to the Headliner. We got somethin' for ya.'

"He knew I was crazy. He went and told his ex-mother-in-law the next day that I pulled a gun on him and that I was crazy, and that her daughter was out of her fuckin' mind to go out with somebody like me. Of course, Denise loved it. Those guys thought they were gonna make fuckin' salami outta me. You should'a seen some of his friends, but that gun was my equalizer. It was a funny story, and when I told it downtown, they just died laughin'.

"I went out with Denise quite a while, and the next thing you know we got married in New Jersey. Who the fuck knows why I did it. It was a city hall wedding, but we had a party after. All the guys from Italian Harlem came, guys from Mulberry Street. We had a nice thing, and then we drove to California.

"You know they say you go to a place to change, but guess what? Wherever you go your baggage goes with you."

In Denise's case, it was a trunk of shoes that traveled with her. For Vince, it was his bad habits... the wrong people, crime, alcohol and drugs.

"And what'd I do in L.A.? I run inta guys in Schwabs from my neighborhood who I either thought were dead or 'on the lam.' We started our own little thing out there—same shit. Then I started with drugs. Denise was a tough little bastard. We were always fightin'. One night, she split for Las Vegas with her friend. She couldn't take me no more. And what I do? I left, too. Packed my shit and I went back to New York.

"I stayed at my father and mother's house, actually, and five days later this trunk pulls up with all her shoes, and it's her, and she's there to stay. Then we were fightin' all the time in my father and mother's two-bedroom house so they threw us out. We went to live with her mother and father, and they threw us out, too. It was always over drinkin' and doin' drugs."

CHAPTER 8

Revenge in Little Italy

In the underworld of Little Italy, there were guys in Vince's crew and associates that were very scary characters, psychopaths even. But this was the life Vince had chosen and he learned to live within it. Among these people newcomers were immediately distrusted, so to be accepted by them was considered an honor.

"There's no trust. That's one thing I noticed in Little Italy. You can be there with me talkin', playin' with your friends and the next minute your friends shoot you."

Blacky Russo was one of the most feared of Vince's associates. He was an out-of-control hothead. "Blacky Russo was like Joe Pesci in the movie *Goodfellows*. But in a way, Blacky made Joe Pesci look like a fuckin' amateur. Blacky was some fuckin' dresser—dressed like a million bucks this guy. There were guys that were pretty boys, and a lot of Italian guys are pretty boys, but Blacky was good lookin' in a real rugged sorta way. He was great with women because he had a real cool way about him."

If Blacky wasn't feared enough, he had a partner named Sammy Pipes, a skinny, extremely skittish loose cannon. Sammy and Blacky were inseparable and a deadly duo for anyone that crossed them.

Everything about Blacky was scary, even his pet. "Blacky had a fuckin' white bulldog, and he usta feed it gunpowder 'cause it made the dog vicious. The dog was vicious enough without the gunpowder. He usta put the gunpowder in the dog's food. This fuckin' dog had pink eyes all the time. What Blacky usta do, the Bowery's not far from Little Italy, when a bum would walk through the neighborhood, he'd go, 'Get 'im!' The dog would run out and attack the poor fuck.

"I made money with Blacky. I didn't act it, but I was petrified; scared to death of this guy."

***

In addition to his criminal activities, Vince held legitimate jobs as well. "I was hangin' down in Little Italy and I was workin' at the Waldorf Astoria as a room clerk. I could get a key to any room. I usta set up rooms for my friends from downtown to rob. If I knew there was a big score in the room, I'd have guys from my neighborhood go up there and take care of business.

"This girl that worked there, Mary O'Brady, who became Mary Bonacorsa, had a boyfriend that was in the service at the time and she says, 'Nicky, when you meet Mikey you guys are gonna hit it off.'

"She introduced me to this guy and his brother was Paulie Bonacorsa. Paulie owned a bar in Astoria, and at the time, I didn't know that he was connected with one of the five families.

"She was right. We hit it off immediately. He had another six months left in the service, and we started talkin' about how to make some money together. And the kid was a natural for con and makin' money."

Vince and Mikey had several scams for making money. "I was using heroin and at that time, Mikey didn't do drugs but we were criminals together. I was the pawn and he was like a big man 'cause his brother was a 'mobbed-up' guy. We had a thing where we would get in his Cadillac at night and drive around rich neighborhoods. This is when I knew I was goin' downhill 'cause my crimes were goin' from top of the line back to the bottom of the line. Whenever, we'd see a rich broad with a pocketbook, I'd jump outta the Cadillac, take the bag, jump back in the Cadillac and we'd take off. So were makin' quite a bit of money like that. If the guys downtown knew about this nickel and dime stuff that would'a been the end; they wouldn't a let me back in the neighborhood."

Vince and Mikey were doing one of these a night. They kept any cash they found and they'd sell the credit cards or anything else they found in the purse.

"It wasn't as sophisticated with credit cards then as it is now. Then you could use them for a while. Today, it's like one, two, three, they can stop everything."

Then Vince and Mikey bought a Tropicana Orange Juice truck route. Mikey bought the truck and the route and Vince was a silent partner.

"Our route was in Harlem. We usta go on the truck with baseball bats and guns because you know we were up there with the blacks, and we were a couple of Italian guys. But we were crazy anyway.

"We had a connection with this black guy at the Armour Food plant in Long Island. Armour Food—like pork, bacon and all that. We'd pay the black guy off, and he'd give us whatever we wanted. This guy was in our pocket. We'd meet him at the back gate at six in the morning, and he would load up our truck with lobster tails and shrimp, and bacon and big slabs of pork. The big thing was the lobster tails. Man, we had lobster tails comin' outta our ass. We'd hit our route up in Harlem, and we're sellin' to every store not only orange juice, but lobster tails and everything else. We'd make a beautiful profit—just with that.

"So I said to the black guy one day, 'Let me ask ya somethin'. What the fuck is the payroll in this joint?'

"He thought about it and said, 'Well ya know, I been watchin' this woman and every week she has a certain exit that she goes to. She takes her car. She goes down this street. She makes a right on that street...' Apparently, this is the woman that did the payroll. Nobody else did it. It was the route that she took every time she went to the bank. So I said to him, 'What the fuck! Why don't ya get this thing mapped out. I can get some guys from downtown. We can pull a beautiful score. How much are we talkin' about?'"

"Maybe a two-hundred fifty thousand dollar hit."

"So I'm thinkin', *What the fuck. This would be paradise. We could do this.*"

Vince and Mikey had to present their plan to the boys downtown before they could proceed. "I bring Mikey with me to Blacky Russo's after hours joint. And Mikey was a pretty cool guy even though he was from Long Island; he was very streetwise. At first Blacky says to me, 'Who's this fuckin' guy?' So I introduced Mikey to him, and said, 'Trust me. He's good people. I could tell ya right now he's a stand-up guy.'

"So Blacky and Sammy Pipes sit down with us and we're drinkin', and we laid the plan out. I knew they were suspicious of Mikey. That's how they are when you bring a new guy downtown—it's like everybody's suspicious. So anyway, we all agree we're gonna do this thing. So we did a dress rehearsal and sure enough the woman did everything she was supposed to do. It was perfect. We set it up to do it the followin' week.

"So the day comes, I got a '45 in my fuckin' belt and meanwhile I had zoned out on a little cocaine, which was my pattern at the time. Sammy, Blacky and Mikey were drinkers and they had a few. Our plan was that she was gonna drive down the street. When she stopped at the stoplight, we were gonna have one car in front of her that was gonna stall, and one in back of her that was gonna stall. We go right to the side of the car and grab the payroll, and she would'a given it up. She would'a never got hurt.

"We go out there and this woman never shows up. So we say, 'What the fuck's goin' on? She's been doin' this forever.' So the wind up is—that day she gets sick and doesn't come to work.

"Now, here I'm doin' this powder like it's goin' outta style and I'm gettin' a little paranoid, right? 'Cause we had it all set up. I got these two fuckin' maniacs with me from downtown that we go all the way to Long Island to do this score and there's no fuckin' score. I got a '45 in my belt under my shirt. It's summertime so my shirt's hanging outta my pants. They got guns under their fuckin' shirts and they were pissed off. I said, 'Hey, look this is gonna happen. Ya know?'"

Like all good Italians when things go wrong, you eat! So Vince and his associates went to eat. But things would become surreal and it wasn't just from the cocaine that Vince was doing.

"We go inta this fuckin' diner. We sit down and there's five fuckin' cops sittin' at the next table. Blacky says in Italian, 'This fuckin' place is full of cops'. We definitely had a plan, and this is no bullshit. If these cops would have come up to us, we were gonna shoot them. It was plain and simple. 'Cause I was fuckin' crazy, high on coke, and Blacky and Sammy were pissed. So we start ordering and I'm sweatin'. It's pourin' out of my fuckin' head 'cause of all the coke. The cops are lookin' at us. They know in their fuckin' hearts that we're trouble, and we're waitin' for them to make a move. This is one of the most dramatic things I ever experienced in my life. It was unbelievable. The four of us all got some fuckin' serious artillery on us, and we're all lookin' at each other. Mikey says under his breath, 'Well, I learned how to fight in Vietnam. This might be our fuckin' time—our day of reckoning.'

"If they would'a come over, we would'a started shootin' and that would'a been it. They get us we get them. I ordered bacon and eggs and we're sittin' there eatin'. I'm shakin' and eatin'. Now, I'm sayin' to myself, *These fuckin' cops are definitely gonna come over*. And the other guys are there tryin' to eat and the cops are there lookin' at us.

"But they didn't come over. We wind up goin' back downtown and guess what? The guys got pissed off at me, and that was nothin' uncommon, and we never put the thing together again. In fact, somethin' happened where we lost the route and that was the end of that. To this day, that time in the diner was the longest half-hour that I ever experienced in my whole fuckin' life."

***

"Another time, we're in Blacky Russo's after hours club, and there's Sammy, Blacky, this kid Barboni, Louie Pisano, Carmine Trufano, and his brother, Benny. And Blacky's breakin' Benny's balls. Carmine and Benny are from the other side, but they got Americanized real quick, and they're both tough kids. So Blacky says somethin' about Benny bein' a greaseball, and he's really givin' it to him. And then, Pipes starts givin' it to him, too. And we're sittin' there, and we're all laughin'. We're havin' a good time. All of a fuckin' sudden, Benny starts throwin' it back at Blacky. And I can see Blacky's whole personality change.

"He went from breakin' Benny's balls to lookin' at Benny like a cat looks at a mouse before he kills it, and poor Benny's goin' on and on. I fuckin' felt it immediately 'cause I knew Blacky. He was crazy. And Benny kept on goin'. The next fuckin' thing, Blacky jumps over the bar. Blacky beat Benny half to death, Carmine, who was a stand-up guy wouldn't make a move. Blacky put this kid in the fuckin' hospital and his jaw had to be wired. He was such a nice kid, a good kid. And for Carmine, it was like he was watchin' his mother get raped.

"I'll tell you somethin' else about my good friend Blacky Russo. I got busted in Wildwood, New Jersey. I shot this kid in the leg by accident 'cause we were on uppers and downers. You know what this cocksucker Blacky does? My friend! He bails me out of the joint and I have to pay 'vig'

70

(interest) on the bail money that he put up for me. My friend! This is a guy that we go inta bars together and I'd pick up the tab, and he had the balls to charge me fuckin' vig on this bail that we got busted on.

"But Blacky finally got his. I came out to L.A. in '71. I was away from the neighborhood for 10 years when my mother died. So I go to New York, and I go down to Little Italy, and who do I see standin' on the corner of Prince Street—Blacky. As usual, he was dressed to kill. He was so happy to see me 'cause I hadn't seen him in years. I told him my mom had passed away. And he said, 'Ah, I'm so sorry to hear that.' Then he says to me with a big smile on his face, 'Hey, I got my button."

"Ya got your button?'

"I wasn't surprised 'cause if there was ever a guy to be made—this fuckin' guy was it. Oh, he was bad news, and I said to him, 'You got made."

"Yeah, I got made. Come on. I'll take ya out ta dinner."

"I went to dinner with him. We talked about this and that, and I sensed somethin' was gonna happen to him. I don't know what it was, somethin' he said, a premonition or what, but I didn't say nothin'. In my head I was thinkin', *Thank God I'm goin' back to California.* Even though I had some crazy friends in California. I said, *Thank God. Thank God I'm goin' back.* I couldn't take this no more.

"Well I got a phone call six months later from Carmine Trufano and he says, 'That cocksucker is dead.'"

"Who?'

"Who? Who the fuck do ya think I'm talkin' about— Blacky. Revenge is sweet!"

"Oh, Blacky was a crazy bastard and he must have been doin' somethin' somebody didn't like, and sure enough six months after I saw him, he got whacked."

CHAPTER 9

Knowing the Right People

Vince acquired a circle of influence among his associates in all five New York Mafia families. Some of these guys were 'lieutenants' and capos. For an up-and-coming guy like Vince, these relationships proved beneficial, yielding work and the kind of connections that could smooth over difficult situations.

"We usta go to the Copa, the Headliner and all the clubs uptown. If you're hangin' out with made guys, even though I wasn't a made guy, when it was time to go out nightclubbin' we'd go out with made guys. We'd be in a nightclub and a lot of times guys would be there that I knew had their button and somebody would say, 'This is a friend of mine,' meaning me; I'm a friend of his. When a made guy meets another made guy they go, 'This is a friend of ours.'

"See, when a guy is made, you don't want somebody that's a friend of his that ain't made to hear certain things. In other words, you're with the made guy and you work for him, but there's things he don't want you to know.

"Me and my friend Paulie—'Fink' they usta call him—Paulie Fink. I don't know why 'cause he was the tightest lipped motherfucker in the world. We were big money 'earners,' and the made guys loved us."

A good earner in the mob is somebody that can put down a big score like robbing a mansion, a jewelry store, a truck hijacking or pulling off a money making scam. "Sometimes they'd hijack a truck, and give us the 'swag' (stolen goods), and we'd deal it out to people we knew. I worked for this guy downtown, Joey Silks on Prince Street. We usta do a lotta swag with him. Our big thing was diamonds. We usta grab diamonds—four, five carat diamonds. It was like a hobby for us."

They would acquire diamonds from assaults on people or home break-ins, and sometimes from jewelry store robberies. A five or six carat diamond ring would yield a considerable amount of money.

"We usta do business in the fourth and sixth ward. The sixth ward is Mulberry Street, Mott Street. The fourth ward is Madison Street and around there. I usta also do business with a guy named 'Slick' in the fourth ward. He was a big guy with the Genovese crew."

Slick was Vince's connection for fencing stolen goods. In the fourth ward, Vince also fenced stolen goods through the Cippolini Brothers.

"Oh, these fuckin' guys—ya talk about Blacky Russo. They made Blacky Russo look like a choirboy. They'd kill their own mother if there was a price tag on her."

So through all this dishonest work Vince made a name for himself and gained respect among the made guys he knew. "Being with made guys meant nobody could fuck with you. But it was all right for the made guys to stick it up our ass when it came down to playin' out the score and givin' us the money. But if somebody tried to fuck with us, the guy's done for. So we had that—and plus it was nice to say, 'Hey, I'm with so and so.' And, I never liked to drop names, but once in a while you had to. I'd say, 'I'm with what's his name.' They'd check you out. Then, when they found out you're with so and so, they'd say, 'Whoa, excuse me. We didn't really mean to say that to ya.' So it was like a protection thing."

Vince usually carried out scores set up by the made guys. "I'm a funny guy. You give me somethin' to do, and I'll do it. But I don't wanna think it up. And I will come up with some things. I remember when I usta do the powder, I'd come up with some ingenious scores. When I was a thief—you could say to me, 'Hey Vince, this is the layout. This is what ya gotta do.' And I'd do it, once you tell me how you want it done. But for me to invent it—I don't know. Most of the time I liked guidance. No matter what the fuck it is. It's very hard for me to say, 'Well I wanna do this or I wanna do that.'

"But I'm not a follower, either. I'm actually a leader type. I have a way of persuadin' people to do what I want and sometimes I'd do it and go over my head. I had the balls to tell anybody if I had a good idea. Even though I don't like to come up with ideas. I like things sometimes to be mapped out for me. I like to be shown. I like you to organize it and I'll do it and do it good. That's the beauty of bein' with those guys. They usta come up with scores that were unfuckin' believable. They'd say Vince, 'We have this job.' And we knew in the end they would fuck us in the ass, but we did it anyway."

There was a downside to many of Vince's friendships. But being well connected as he was, meant that these guys were there to help.

"Made guys could get you outta messes when things went wrong."

Payoffs could be made to police and District Attorneys to look the other way or to misplace evidence. Judges could be paid off to drop charges, or to plea bargain to a lesser offense. Even when that wasn't possible, a judge could be convinced to come up with a more lenient sentence, or even probation. Which usually meant the individual would be back out on the street and back in business, again.

***

One of Vince's more successful money making schemes came about one night in Little Italy. He was hanging around with the Vincenzo brothers.

"We're sittin' down in 'Danny Boy' Vincenzo's 'card club' on Twelfth Street. Mickey 'Bones,' Danny Boy's brother just got outta the federal joint. Danny wasn't workin', and he was livin' on Mickey's reputation. Danny was a good earner but he was lazy. He had this card club, and it wasn't makin' any fuckin' money, and he was dyin'. So I said to him, 'What the fuck. This is a nickel and dime joint. I know these guys that have a band. Why don't we do this—Friday night we get the band in here, and we have like a little dance. We put a bar up, and we have a fuckin' night club.'

"Danny thought it over and Mickey said, 'Ya got the band. Ya got my name.' So we made this inta a dancin' thing on Friday night, then Saturday night, too. It became an after-hours club. I became a partner 'cause it was my idea. It was a phenomenon, and we made a fortune. Every week we were makin' thousands of fuckin' dollars.

"The cops came around and they're gettin' money, too. But after a while, they burnt us out. They wanted more and more, every week. So we closed it down, but we had a good thing goin' for a couple of months. Not to say the pussy we had in there. We had this two-way mirror in the bathroom. The girls, whenever they went in we'd go behind the mirror. You'd be surprised what girls do in front of mirrors. You think guys are somethin'. Guys ain't shit compared to girls."

Eventually, Danny got pissed off at Vince because "Mickey was startin' to take to me, and he made a remark to Danny one night, he said, 'This fuckin' kid—he ain't even from the neighborhood and he can make me more money than you can make me.' I was sorry he said that 'cause Danny was a jealous cocksucker. Danny stuttered. He usta go, 'Ja, ja, ja, ja...' You know, this cocksucker had me stutterin' after a while. If you hang around with a stutterer long enough, you start stutterin' too."

Danny and Mickey had another brother named Ralphy. He was the honest one in the family. "One night Ralphy was talkin' about his job in the coffee warehouse, and I'm thinkin' warehouse. That was in the days when they usta pay you in cash. They'd put the money in a 'boosta' (money in an envelope).' There was none of this check shit. So I said to Ralphy, 'How'da ya get paid in this fuckin' joint?'

"And he says, 'Every Friday, everybody goes ta lunch and when everybody's at lunch this guy fills envelopes.' There were a hundred fuckin' workers. 'Then he puts 'em on their desk and when everybody comes back from lunch they got their pay.'

"So right away my antenna went up and I said, "Ralphy!" I looked at Mickey and he looked at me and then he went like ya know, this guy, faget it, Ralphy ain't gonna do it. And I said to Ralphy, 'What kind of a layout is this?'

"Ralphy knew what I was up to. He said, 'Nicky (aka, Vince), this is my fuckin' job.'

"I said, 'How much are we fuckin' talkin' about here?"

"There's about 20–25 grand."

"So I said, 'Fuck, that's a good little hit.'

"So after that night—I did somethin' I could'a got killed for. I called Mickey. I said, 'Mickey, your brothers don't wanna do this.' Oh, I was an instigatin' bastard, and I said, 'They don't gotta do nothin'. I'll do this myself. Ya set this fuckin' thing up for me and I'll go down and do it.'"

Mickey convinced his brothers to let Vince pull the job. "This was right by the Brooklyn Bridge in lower Manhattan. Ralphy gave us the layout—it was perfect. There's the office. There's a solid black door in the front of the office. There's another door like that on the side, and you gotta go inta the hallway to get to the side door. The guy would keep the side door open. The door in the front is closed but not locked, 'cause you don't wanna be makin' out envelopes with people walkin' by.

"We figured the whole thing out and went through all the logistics. So Ralphy says, 'The guy sits down and he has about five grand in his fuckin' pocket. He definitely always has that money in his pocket. The safe is open, and he's makin' out the fuckin' envelopes. There should be about 15 grand just in the safe alone, plus the envelopes. Ya can make about, maybe, 35 grand on this one if ya do it.'

"Now Ralphy the honest brother, was inta it too. Mickey is the made guy. I thought of it, but Mickey put it out, so he said, 'Ralphy, ya get a 'tipster's end.' Sally, ya drive. Nicky, ya do the score.'

"I said, 'Beautiful!'

"So I dressed like a locksmith with the name of this locksmith company on my shirt. I had a phony mustache. They had makeup on me and a big nose. So we go down there and I go in. It was perfect. I walk through the side door. I tell the guy, 'Hey, I'm so and so from the locksmith company. There's somethin' wrong with your lock.' Now, as I'm doin' this, I close the door behind me and I go to the front door and lock it.

"The guy says, 'What're ya talkin' about?' I pull this '45, handcuff the guy and tape his mouth. There was a woman in there, too. She has a big fuckin' rock on her finger. I see her throwin' the fuckin' ring under the radiator. I ignore it and taped her, too. I say, 'Don't worry, nobody's gonna get hurt. I just want the money.'

"I always tried to make people feel comfortable. I never hurt anybody. I go to the fuckin' safe. There's about ten fuckin' grand in there. I grab the envelopes and put them in my fuckin' beach bag. This score is poetry in fuckin' motion. This was a forty fuckin' large score, and I did it in five minutes. Oh, yeah, and I got the ring, too. I did it real cute. I went under the radiator, and said, 'Oooh, look at this,' and I picked it up and threw it in the bag."

Then everything fell apart for Vince. "I walked out the front door, and there's a fuckin' cop facin' me. He saw somethin' in me. I didn't know what it was, and he says, 'Hey, I wanna talk to you!'

"He made a move towards me. I went in the bag to get the '45 and he put the drop on me. He would'a popped me and he would'a got me good. I would'a been a dead man. So

I dropped the bag. I bet this cocksucker was probably made detective after that.

"Up until then it was a perfect fuckin' score, and I got 'busted.' Then I find out that there were cops all around that fuckin' area. Some fuckin' guy was throwin' himself off the Brooklyn Bridge. He was up on the bridge, on top of the fuckin' railin', and I get busted. I wound up in the Raymond Street Jail. But this is the good part, where knowin' the right people comes in—they get me a good lawyer. They got me this and that. Some favors were rollin'. You know—crooked shit—and I got away with it. See, in New York they're all crooked bastards. This is where knowin' wise guys came in very handy. They squashed it.

"And you wanna know how sick I was? My thought was: *I wanted to shoot this cop*, but he was faster than me. And it's funny, I walked out there real normal, but he saw somethin', even though I looked like a locksmith. I panicked when he said, 'Hey!' And, I wanted to find out who this guy was who was commitin' suicide because I wanted to kill him, too. Ya talk about denial. I wanted to get this prick because if it wasn't for him I would'a walked outta there with the money. I really wanted to get the fuckin' score done 'cause I wanted Mickey to fuckin' notice me big time. Oh, I wanted to get made. I had eyes on gettin' made so bad."

This was another time when Vince made sure he had enough alcohol in him to have the courage to do the job.

CHAPTER 10

My Friend Anthony

Vince had other friends in Little Italy besides the Vincenzos, Blacky Russo, Sammy Pipes, and their kind. People he trusted and really cared about. One of these guys was his good friend Anthony. Anthony grew up and lived in Little Italy.

"He was an Italian kid, and he looked like an angel. He looked like a clean cut college kid, but he dressed like a hood."

Besides being young good-looking guys, Vince and Anthony were big spenders, and they dressed to kill in their tailor made mohair suits, alligator shoes, and on their pinky finger they sported large diamond rings. They were the kind of guys hip New York girls went for. Anthony and Vince had a weekly ritual of bar hopping to meet girls and then double dating.

"We made a good team. We always met girls Friday night, and then Saturday night, we'd date them. Well, this was goin' on for a couple of years, and me and Anthony, we were really tight. I'd go over his house, and he'd come over mine."

One Friday night they met two girls from Staten Island. "Boy, I liked this girl, Italian girl. And Anthony met her friend, but he wasn't that impressed with her friend, but I really liked this girl. This one really hit the mark and we hit it off right away. Durin' the week I called and told her, 'I'd like to take ya out on Saturday night.'

"She said, 'Saturday night, we got a wedding to go to, but you know what? I'd like my family to meet ya. How about ya come over my house on Friday night? My mother's gonna make a big Italian dinner. And ya come over and meet my family.'

"Wow! I like that, but ya know, usually me and Anthony go out on Friday night."

Vince thought about it a moment and said, "I'll tell Anthony; we'll just switch it around. Friday night, he can go out on a date, and Saturday night him and I'll hang out together."

After hanging up, Vince called Anthony and told him about his plans. "And I fig'a he's gonna say to me, 'That's good. What the fuck. Beautiful. Ya go out and Saturday night we'll hook up.'"

But instead of openly accepting Vince's suggestion, "He fuckin' gets inta this shit with me, 'Well, ya know, we always do Friday night. We always go out.'

"I said, 'I like this fuckin' broad. Give me a break. I wanna go out with her.'"

"Yeah, but why don't ya tell her that ya'll go out with her next week?"

"Hey Anthony, not for fuckin' nothin', but I'm gonna go out to her house in Staten Island and have a nice dinner. Ya go out with her fuckin' friend, or do what the fuck ya want, and tomorrow night we'll go out together.

"He's goin' on and on. I was ready to start a fuckin' fight with this guy. 'Cause, I had a hot temper, and I'm thinkin', *Go fuck yourself!*

"Finally, he says, 'Awright. Awright, we'll do that.'

"He was pissed off. I thought Jesus Christ, I'm not married to this fuckin' guy. But that's the way he took it. So Friday night, I go out to see this girl. It was beautiful. I met the mother and father. We ate dinner. It was nice. So next morning my eyes open up, and I felt guilty. Let me call this fuckin' kid so tonight we can go out. I call his house and his mother answered the phone. In her broken English she says, 'Nicky, Nicky!' She's hysterical and cryin' her fuckin' eyes out.

"I could hardly understand her. I said, 'Signora. Signora. What, what? What happened?'

"They kill Anthony. They kill Anthony."

"Who killed Anthony?"

"Of course, she didn't know who killed him and the poor woman was heartbroken. They found Anthony parked up in the Bronx, sitting in the driver's seat of his car with two bullets in the back of his head.

"I didn't know who did it, either. So after that conversation with his mother, I'm scared. She's hysterical, and I'm thinkin', *Holy shit they whacked him*, and I didn't even know the reason they whacked him. I'm thinkin', *I'm his best friend. They're gonna whack me, too*. So right away I go down to the sixth ward, and I talk to this guy, Rico DiCello, who's on Prince Street. Joey Silks is with him. I tell Rico, 'Look, I don't wanna get hit. I didn't do a fuckin' thing. And if ya think for one minute the word is out on me... I'm a civilian almost. I'm not a made guy. I'm not lookin' for no fuckin' trouble.'

"Joey Silks says, 'Ah, Nicky, you're a good kid.'"

"Please, whoever took him out. Let the word go out I'm not lookin' for revenge."

"I kept away from the neighborhood for two weeks after that."

The memory of Anthony and how he died would always remain an open wound for Vince.

CHAPTER 11

Fighting at the Headliner

His years in Coxsackie, the many fights he had there and the extreme punishment he endured as a result, didn't cure Vince of fighting. The life he chose to live and the people he chose to hang around with lived violent lives and fights were a big part of it. Ironically, fighting didn't sit well with the people he most wanted to impress—the lieutenants and capos he worked for.

"I wanna be a made guy. But here's my problem. I drink, go inta clubs, and I start fights. So now the word is gettin' out. 'OK, Vince is good. He does this. He does that. He's a good earner. We like ya Vince. You're a good guy. Ya got balls of a lion.' But they're pushin' me away. In other words, we'll let ya get close to us, but we ain't gonna let ya get that close.

"Year's later, a girl in 'AA' told me, 'You know why you didn't get made? You don't get made if you're an alcoholic and a drug addict. What are you gonna say, 'Hey guys, it was nice doing business with you, but I'm goin' into AA now, and I'm gonna quit the family.'

"They'll whack you. Some of the guys I knew that got made were Mickey Mouse guys. They were buyin' their buttons. I thought I earned mine, but it never happened."

And what happenend at the Headliner Club probably didn't help Vince's cause at all. The club in Midtown Manhattan where he and his friends hung out was the scene of an outrageous brawl.

"So we're in the Headliner one night. We were fuckin' big sports. Dressed to kill. Friends of ours from Harlem were there, too. They were good people. We even did a little work with some of them.

"So I'm with Denise. All the girls we knew were there. We're drinkin' and we're havin' a good time. Now, I understand how we all became alcoholics. You're in a bar, somebody says, 'Buy 'im a drink.' Somebody else says, 'Buy 'im a drink.' You usta have seven, eight drinks lined up. What the fuck you gonna do with them? Somebody else says, 'Buy those guys a drink!'

"Everyone's tryin' to outdo everyone else. So you got all these drinks, everybody's gettin' fucked up. All of a sudden, this guy from Harlem tried somethin' with a downtown girl, and she went and told her brother who was there. The next fuckin' thing you know words were said and everybody's hittin' one another. Before you know it, there's 45 guys fightin' just like that—over a fuckin' girl!

"It was like somebody pushed a button. All these guys from Harlem and all these guys from Little Italy we're swingin' at each other. This kid Bruno picks an axe off the fuckin' wall, and he hits this fuckin' kid, called Nose from Harlem over the fuckin' head. Bruno was famous with axes. He loved them.

"Guys were gettin' hit with bottles. Every fuckin' bottle was gone from the bar. I mean you wanted to see a fight. You ain't never seen nothin' like this in your life. We were beautifully dressed in our silk suits and alligator shoes. Suits were ripped, blood all over the place. When we walked outta that club, it looked like somebody put us through a trash compactor. The club was a fuckin' shambles. It was destroyed that night. We got hurt. A few guys from Harlem got hurt. Everybody was fucked up. And these were our friends. That's how sick it all was."

That was only the beginning. Vince and his friends would have to reckon with the owners of the Headliner. The fighters would each be summoned to the social club of the Harlem mob and the social club of the Little Italy mob.

These clubs were usually non-descript storefronts with blacked-out windows where mob guys hung out and conducted business over a cup of espresso or a glass of wine. There was no espresso or wine being served to the participants in the fight when they came to the clubs.

"We got called up to the club on 107th Street in Harlem. Jo Jo Argenteri was the capo up there at the time. I was good friends with his daughter. My other friend Johnny Randazzo—we usta hang out in Long Beach together—his father was there, too. His father loved me. But it didn't matter who we were friends with.

"It was not just we go up to Harlem. A week later they call you downtown. And it's more humiliation. They don't just hit you. They talk to you first. They come up to you. They talk to you real low. They walk around you, and then they hit you. Sometimes they hit you with a bat. They hit you with whatever they want—you gotta take it. They didn't beat us. That we could take. Most of the time they smacked us. And I'm the type of guy—you smack me, I'm gonna fight you. I just couldn't. If you raised your hands they'll shoot you. Oh, yeah. You didn't fight back. Oh no, they'll roll you out in a carpet. No one'll ever see you again. They want you to do that. Oh, and they talked to us like we were pieces of shit. 'You scumbag, fuckin' low life, cocksucker.' They told us they didn't know how we were gonna do it, but we were gonna make up for everything that was destroyed in the Headliner. We were gonna pay for it all.

"And the guys from Harlem had to go to the Harlem club and the club in Little Italy. Even the guys whose father's were made guys had to go. And they got smacked around in both places. Oh, yeah. They don't care that you're a tough guy. They don't care that we made money with them. They didn't give a fuck. They humiliated us. Oh, you're gonna get hurt and disgraced.

"But we had about 60 guys all makin' good money, and they all chipped in. After a while, it was paid off and the

Headliner reopened. And how'd it all start? Over a fuckin' girl! Well, why not? How many fights in bars did you ever see that weren't over a girl? Every bar you go to—you drink—there's a girl involved—there's a fight."

CHAPTER 12

My Not So Glamorous Life

Each day, Vince's life became more and more influenced by drugs and less by his mob associates. He lived a double life. There were his friends that he did heroin with and there were his friends that he made money with. Some of them were the same people. For instance, Tony Mastretti was one of his heroin shooting buddies. Mas was also Johnny Goomba's right hand man, and Goomba didn't do drugs. In fact, he disdained them and would have killed Vince and Mas if he knew they were on heroin. Back then, drugs were considered a source of income for the mob and not something they used themselves. Drinking was by far the popular intoxicant among mob guys. Many times Vince was high on drugs while sitting with his associates in one of the social clubs.

"Talk about playin' the actor. They thought I was a little slow."

"Whatta fuck's a matta with ya? Don't ya ever sleep?"

"I was really gettin' down to the point where the glamorous part of my life was goin' down the toilet. One cold, snowy night, I went uptown to one of the brownstones on 55th and 9th Avenue to score some heroin. I went up the steps and this Puerto Rican guy opens the door and slips me three, 'nickel bags' of heroin. I paid him and as I'm walkin' down the steps a fuckin' patrol car pulls up. The cop says, 'Hey, kid! Whatta you doin'?'

"Nothin'."

"Come over here!"

"And I knew what he was gonna do. He was gonna get me over there and frisk me, and they would'a found the three nickels that I had. So I went to go towards him, then turned and started to run. I could run in those days, snow and everything. And I'm runnin' and runnin'. I turn at the corner, then another corner, and another. I'm runnin' and I see a wall. I say fuck! That's it. I'm gonna jump over this wall, and I'm gonna hide, and them motherfuckers'll just keep on goin'."

Vince's plan worked; he eluded the police but was in for a big surprise. "I figa'd it was a small jump. I jumped over the fuckin' wall, and I still got this heroin in my hand. I'm goin' down and down and down. I didn't know it but it was four stories down. On the way down, I fuckin' hit the wall with my foot just to break the fall, and I came down hard in a pile of snow. Fortunately, there was enough snow to keep me from killin' myself. But I hit the concrete with my head and knocked out two teeth.

"You would think that I would say 'oh my God—look what I fuckin' did.' But, no, I crawled outta the snow inta this little hallway, down the alley, and opened up the three bags of heroin and 'snorted' them. I laid there all fuckin' night high, in the freezin' cold. The next day, I don't know how I managed to get the fuck outta there. I went home to my parents house. I was still high.

"My mother looked at me, shook her head and said, 'Oh, madone.'

"The only important thing in my life at that time was those three bags of heroin. I never thought that I could'a broken every fuckin' bone in my body."

***

Eventually, Vince's drug usage became so bad that his own mother, realizing the extent of his addiction, turned him in to the authorities. "I wound up in Creedmore State Hospital for the criminally insane. They put me up on the top floor with all the crazies. I was supposed to be there for two weeks. It turned inta a year."

After Vince was committed, they diagnosed him with hepatitis. Ironically, he believes he contracted hepatitis from a dirty needle while shooting up with his estranged wife Denise's ex-husband Ronny. The same character that Vince drew a gun on a couple of years earlier on Broadway.

"Yeah, Ronny and I eventually became shootin' buddies. He was goin' out with a black girl that was a friend of mine. She told me she was with Ronny."

One night when Vince was with her, Ronny came over. "He shit when he saw me, and I said, 'Ah, forget about it. Ya wanna 'get loaded?' We got some dope. We shot up with one of his needles, and it must have been infected with hepatitis.

"I was dyin' from the hepatitis. I weighed ninety pounds. I was so weak, couldn't eat anythin'. You could'a blown me over. The priest came in to give me last rites. I said, 'Ya ain't givin' me shit father. I ain't goin' nowhere.'"

The medications they put Vince on eventually helped him to pull through. "That was a bad one, the worst. I should of realized then that there's a God up there."

***

Throughout this period of Vince's life, his troubles with Denise continued. He couldn't get free of her.

"I wouldn't go back with her and she wouldn't divorce me. It took me five years to get rid of her. We were at the end of our relationship. It was a crazy situation. It was like a love-hate thing. We knew it was bad. She'd go and fuck around, and I'd be broken-hearted, and then she'd catch me with some girl and she'd go crazy. It was fuckin' insanity.

"Once we were in Wildwood, New Jersey. Me and all the guys were out at the pool takin' the sun. She was on the second floor with this stupid wig on. She was inta wigs then. She called me, 'Nicky, come up!' She was high on somethin'. 'If ya don't come up here I'm gonna throw myself off the fuckin' balcony.'

"Carmine Trufano says to her, 'Do it and shut the fuck up!'

"Then one night, she really got me good. She had me jumped outside the Kearney Yacht Club. She was hangin' around with these girls from 'Down Neck,' near Newark. So one night at the club I'm with this little girl Linda Palermo. Linda was a hairstylist that worked in Union, New Jersey. Hannibal and the Head Hunters were playin' that night. Ya know the song, 'Nah, nah, nah, nah, nah...'

"Denise says to me, 'Nicky, would ya come outside? I wanna talk to ya.' And I looked at her as if what the fuck ya mean. Can't ya see I'm with a girl? And Linda was a pretty cool girl. She knew about Denise. She says, 'Why don't ya go out and get it over with? Take care of it and come back.'

"So I go outside and I start talkin' to her. And as I'm talkin' to her, I look around me—there's six guys around me. Guys from Silver Lake, near Newark, her friends. She had set me up to catch a fuckin' beatin'. I had on an Italian knit shirt, these beautiful forest green mohair pants, green alligator shoes, a white leather, handmade three-quarter length jacket, the pinky ring and the hat."

Guys, then, used to wear small brimmed fedora hats like the ones the Blues Brothers wore.

"As soon as I saw these guys, I knew what was goin' down. So I fig'a I'm gonna hit the biggest one, and go at it. I was pretty fast with my hands. I hit this guy Fats. The same Fats that was with Ronny the night I pulled the gun on them. It was like hittin' a refrigerated side of beef in a meat locker. Thud. I said, oh my God. Then they started beatin' me. I fell down and they were kickin' me. When they were finished, everything I had on looked like I went through a shredder. I was layin' there in pain. I couldn't walk. I had nobody with me except Linda. Nobody! Usually, I went up there with around eight, nine guys. The guys liked to fool around with the Jersey girls. I was by myself that night and they beat the shit outta me.

"The next day Denise calls. She's cryin' and she tells me, 'Oh, I just feel so bad about what they did to ya.'

"I said, 'If ya were a guy, right now ya'd be dead. Your the one that set me up.'"

"I didn't want it to turn out like that and they just started hittin' ya."

"Ya know what Denise? I got nothin' to say to ya."

"She called me five times. I kept hangin' up. But I did tell her, 'Call your friends. Tell them within this year they're gone. They're all gone. Ya tell them.' And ya know what? I went downtown and my friends saw what happened to me, too."

The code of the street dictated that Vince's friends were obligated to revenge his honor.

"She told her father, too, and her father calls downtown. Now her father is a Lucchese guy. I'm with Genovese guys from downtown, around Prince Street. When he found out who I was with, he said to his people, 'If this kid wants to fuck these guys up, ya don't say a fuckin' word, and there's nothin' ya can do about it. Every one of those guys that beat him up is fair game.'"

Vince got his revenge. Him and his friends returned beatings to each of the guys that beat him up that night.

"It took me over a year. Got two of them down the Jersey Shore. We got a couple of them at a bowling alley out in Silver Lake. We caught one at a dance. One by one, we got them all. That guy Fats, too. He was one of the biggest guys, and he was the one we really gave it to. And my friend, Blacky Russo, was involved in this. Hey, they jumped my ass. He just returned the favor."

CHAPTER 13

The Lovely Cheryl

Vince resumed his drug use shortly after his release from Creedmore and eventually got his divorce from Denise. One night at an uptown nightclub he met Cheryl, who would become his next wife.

"It was back in the day when everybody was hangin' outside the clubs, doing pills, coke and shit. The night we met we really had a wild time together. In fact, I dropped some acid, and I never dropped acid again. See I never believed in hallucinogenics, or pot, peyote, and all that shit. But that night, I wanted to try it, and it was a weird trip… it was pretty wild. I didn't like that stuff."

Cheryl was different from the tough mob groupies that Vince was used to going out with. She wasn't Italian. She was from Barbados, a working girl from a good Irish family.

"She was a secretary on Wall Street. Cheryl was a knockout, pretty, a little 'zaftig' with a beautiful face."

Vince and Cheryl spent that entire night together. "We had a sexy thing goin', and after that night, we started goin' out."

Vince was so much in love with Cheryl that it started to affect his criminal activities. Guilt started to creep into his consciousness for the first time. One night outside a club, he noticed an expensive black Mercedes parked with an attractive girl who was dealing coke from the car.

"The money was flyin', and the coke was flyin', too."

Vince got friendly with her and after a while she invited him into the car and the two started making out. But sex wasn't on Vince's mind that night. He was more interested in the wad of cash she had been collecting all night. When the moment was right, he hit her with a right to the jaw and stole her money.

"Afterwards, I went home and for an hour I scrubbed myself in the shower. I felt like I was scrubbin' dirt off me. After that I went to see Cheryl. I felt bad that I hit the girl. I couldn't look Cheryl in the face because I loved her and I felt guilty about what I did."

This wasn't the first time Vince had hit a girl, but somehow Cheryl's influence over him had a profound affect.

"I'm not proud to say this. I come from a family of hitters. And as a kid, I was hit a lot and I hit back. I hit my folks back when I couldn't take it no more. I'm not gonna let people hit me. See that's what happens when you come from a family where you see hittin' all the time. And I knew a lot of Italian guys from my crew that if a woman got out of line, they'd smack them. Back in the day, I usta go out with a lot of bimbos. And if we felt like they got out of line, you'd give them a smack. Most of the girls we went out with that you smacked—they'd try to smack you back. I hung out with some really vile girls. but I'm not proud of that. Every time I did things like that I felt demoralized. In my heart, I always felt like I was a good person. I'd act like a decent human being until you did somethin' that annoyed me, and I'd attack you."

After he met Cheryl, little changes began to occur in Vince's life. He knew things couldn't continue the way they were going. The people he was doing business with began to make him more and more uncomfortable, and it could have been his own paranoia from the result of his out of control drug use.

"I was doin' a lot of 'black beauties' in those days, which were uppers."

He was living at home with his parents and the little time that he did spend there was fraught with turmoil and constant arguments until his parents finally threw him out.

At that point, he went to live with Cheryl and her parents. "Her parents were pretty liberal. They let me sleep with her in her bedroom. I was thinkin' how the fuck can they let me do that, me bein' an old-fashioned Italian and all. But I went with the program because we all got along."

Family harmony was something unfamiliar to Vince. There was never any harmony in his relationship with his parents so this was a new life for him. As usual, he was unaware that he had reached another turning point in his life. It was Cheryl's positive influence in his life. He was in love for the second time in his life. After a while, Vince and Cheryl decided to get married.

"We got married in a church in New York, and then we flew out to Los Angeles. That's when we lived on Fuller Avenue in Hollywood."

This was the second and final time that Vince moved to California. He left his New York life behind to start a new life with Cheryl in Hollywood. But he immediately fell back in with some of his old buddies that had also left behind the turbulent streets of New York for the sunshine of Southern California. They all hung out at Schwab's Drug Store, the infamous place at Sunset and Crescent Heights Boulevards, where supposedly the young Lana Turner was discovered at the counter.

Before too long, he was involved in the same illegal activities with his friends—and drugs and alcohol were a constant part of it. "When I got there, I had money from all the shit I was doin' back East. Of course, Cheryl started workin' right away. She got a good job as a secretary, and I usta lay around the pool where we lived. I would sit by the pool and in the course of a day drink a gallon of fuckin' wine 'cause the manager of our place usta go to the winery and bring me back six one gallon bottles. I'd fuckin' polish them off in a week. It's amazin'… I never realized that I had a problem with alcohol. I just laid by the pool, got a tan and drank. I didn't wanna do shit. I worked as a bartender back East, but I didn't want to do that in L.A."

Unfortunately, Vince's marriage to Cheryl was doomed from the start. "It only lasted four years. Cheryl didn't want a divorce. She wanted to stay with me. "But I knew it wasn't workin' out." The two remained friends after the split up.

CHAPTER 14

A Legitimate Occupation

Life hadn't changed much for Vince in Hollywood. It was a new environment but he had brought all his bad habits and old emotional baggage with him. He didn't realize it at the time but something was subconsciously gnawing at him—what to do with the rest of his life. The solution to which was not far off.

"Then one day it happened. I was walkin' down Hollywood Boulevard with Cheryl and we got to the corner of Las Palmas and Hollywood Boulevard and there was a barber college. All of a sudden, I fuckin' went crazy. It was like I hit the lottery. I jumped up and down and yelled, 'Ah, this is it Cheryl!'"

"What?"

"This is it! I'm gonna be a hairstylist."

"And that was it. I just went with that and I never stopped. Back East, I worked for a wig place. I usta comb them out. Once, they had the audacity to try and make me cut one and I destroyed it. Maybe that's what got me interested in cuttin' hair."

Or, it could have been the many hours Vince had spent as a child watching his father cut hair that made him want to do the same thing.

"I found myself actually enjoin' watchin' him. I was fascinated with the way he cut hair and he was a good haircutter. You know, they say kids follow in their parents footsteps, even though they don't want to, they sponge up a lot of what their parents do.

"My father never wanted me to be a barber. He wanted me to be an architect. But bein' a barber in those days—I mean, my poor dad—I don't think he ever made more than $200 in a week cuttin' hair. That was the old days. Today, you can make $200 in a half-day cuttin' hair. He wanted me to do more with my life. But thank God I became a barber. I probably would'a stayed the way I was and never accomplished nothin'. 'Cause I sure as hell wasn't good in school."

Vince plunged into his new education with his usual zeal. "Oh, it was a fuckin' beautiful thing. They make you an apprentice for twelve months, then they give you an apprentice license, then you're able to work in a shop for another year. After that, you gotta go back to school and take the whole fuckin' exam all over again. You gotta start over like a beginner, do the written test, the oral test, the whole thing. But now it's different, it's a one shot exam and that's it."

Vince successfully completed barber school and went to work. But it wasn't in one of the fashionable Beverly Hills or Brentwood hairstyling establishments.

"I've always been a ghetto kid so where do I go to work, down on Alvarado Street." (Alvarado Street is one of L.A.'s ghetto areas located close to downtown.) "And how befittin', 'cause on Alvarado Street, there were drugs down there, and cute lookin' Mexican women."

Vince felt right at home in this neighborhood. His next job was a step up, a slightly better neighborhood but not by much. "I went to work at Jeremy's down on Berendo Street."

That's where Vince gave me my first haircut. The shop was in a little strip mall with five or six storefronts of different enterprises. The neighborhood was a lower-to-middle class area, just one block behind the tall office buildings of Mid-Wilshire Boulevard, and just a few minutes from downtown L.A.

Vince loved his new profession, a profession that he continues to do today. As a customer of his for more than thirty years, I can vouch that he'll give you the best haircut you'll ever get. He is so meticulous that he'll cut the same area of your head over and over again. Then, just when you think he's finished he'll return to that same spot, or some other place on your head for an indefinite amount of time. One of his customers put it best when he said, "Your haircut is finished when Vince says it's finished."

In his new profession he started to make honest money for the first time in his life and really enjoyed the work. But his life wouldn't change that much. He was still not satisfied.

"It wasn't enough for me."

He was still attracted to drugs, crime and all the wrong people. "In my mind, I still wanted to be a tough guy."

In fact, working on Berendo Street put him in contact with the kind of people that would advance those ambitions.

"Well one day, this Cuban guy comes in with his body guard, and I cut his hair. And I knew right away he was a tough guy, just by the way he dressed. And after that first haircut, he comes back the second time and he says his name is Manny Ramirez. He says, 'Hey, ju like cocaine?'"

"Shit yeah, I like cocaine." It was the seventies.

"Ho-kay, I just wan'ed ta know."

"Next time he comes in, he brings me in a tin foil with a chunk of cocaine. I made about 30 grams outta that fuckin' thing. And you know—he started to like me. And then he says to me, 'Ju hang out with those New York guys?'"

"I said, 'Yeah.' He happened to run inta them and they mentioned my name. And these guys said, 'This fuckin' guy's good people.'"

"So when Manny came back again for a haircut, he said, 'Ju wanna make some money with me?'"

"Sure."

"Move some powder fer me."

"Ya got it."

"So I started movin' powder. Started with ounces, then kilos. I wasn't even touchin' it. I was puttin' it in other people's hands. I was a broker. I was puttin' the Italians together with the Cubans."

So Vince's new profession paid off two-fold. He was earning a good living as a hairstylist and he was doubling his income selling drugs.

CHAPTER 15

Adventures Overdosing

One of the greatest risks for any drug user is overdosing. Overdosing on drugs like heroin and even cocaine can be fatal. Who knows what long-term effects "ODing" has on the body. On more than one occasion, Vince overdosed on heroin and cocaine.

"I 'ODed' in New York one time. I shot some cocaine in between my toes, and I thought I was dead. It was so powerful that I fell to my knees. I made it out of there by myself. Another time I shot dope [heroin] in New York up on a rooftop, and I ODed'. I wound up in Belleview that time. I don't know who brought me there, and I lived through that one, too."

While living in his Fuller Avenue apartment in Hollywood, Vince overdosed on heroin again. "My friend Charlie and I were dealin' cocaine. Charlie got involved with the Mexican guys, and they got us this heroin. It's like black tar. It smells like coffee grinds and comes in chunks. You think it's hashish, but it's heroin."

Heroin in New York was called China White because it was a pure white powder. Mexican heroin at that time in L.A. was called Mexican brown or brown sugar as in the Rolling Stones' song. Today, most of the heroin on the streets of L.A. is white. It usually comes from poppies from Iran and Afghanistan and gets here via Europe.

"So, Charlie comes up to my apartment and he says, 'Oh, I want you to field test this for me.'

"He didn't know how to shoot up or nothin'. He was a 'snorter.' So I just cooked a little up for him. I shot him up with it, and he felt it. Then I shot up a little and I felt it. But I

103

said, *Fuck, if he could shoot a little, I can shoot a lot more than that.* So I put a little more on the cooker and I shot up. The next thing you know, I'm down at L.A. County Hospital lookin' up at the lights, a doctor and four cops, and they're all lookin' down at me. It was a weird feelin' lookin' up at them."

But Charlie saved Vince's life by calling 911. The emergency medical team revived Vince. "I fig'a God must have had a purpose for me. It was the third or fourth time in my life that I was saved from either gettin' stabbed, shot or ODing.

"So I'm lookin' up at them. I'm feelin' okay. I go to get up to leave and the cop pushes me back down and says, 'You ain't goin' nowhere.'"

"Whatta ya mean?"

"You're under arrest."

"For what?"

"For 'marks.' For 'internal possession.'"

"What?"

"That's right."

"See, in New York if you got marks on your arm they don't do nothin', but in L.A. if you got marks or internal possession they can arrest you. I did 90-days in the county jail for that. I did a few county jail stints in L.A. This is the funny part. Everything I got busted for in L.A. was Mickey Mouse stuff—holes in my arms, internal possession... The big stuff, if they would'a caught me, you would'a never seen me again—the coke dealin', the stolen airline tickets and credit cards."

As a result of the marks charge Vince became good friends with a Mexican bail bondsman who was in the Mexican Mafia. "I was involved with the boys in L.A. People met with people, and I met Mexican guys that the bail bondsman was connected with."

That relationship led Vince into becoming a middleman for drug deals between his Italian friends and the Mexican

Mafia. Vince's other connection with the Mexican mob was through a Mexican girl named Lisa that his friend Charlie introduced him to.

"We met at a club, and the next thing you know, I'm dancin' with her. She knows I'm hooked up with the guys, and we started talkin'. She says, 'Well you know, I need coke.'

"I said, 'Well I can use some heroin.'

"She could get me all the heroin I wanted, and I could get her all the coke she wanted. I hooked up with her friends, and we're makin' money, and that's how it works. I was a broker. Towards the end, I started tappin' inta the supply for my own habit, waterin' it down. That's what happens when you're a user.

"Actually, I saved her life once. She and I had shot a little heroin. She passed out and turned blue. I threw her in the bathtub, and put ice all over her body. Her fuckin' friends wanted to let her die. I said, 'You fuckin' motherfuckers.'

"These girls were from heavy people [Mexican Mafia]. They said, 'Fuck her.'"

"What are ya crazy?"

"I thought, *Maybe these Mexican people they treat each other like that*. I didn't know, but I couldn't see her dyin'. That was bullshit. So, I saved her life. She knew it afterwards. In fact she told me, 'Wow, I owe you for savin' my life.'"

***

One day Vince would experience a big surprise when his old friend Mikey Bonacorsa called him from New York. "I was livin' in L.A. and dabblin' with heroin on the weekends. I get this phone call from Mikey and he wants to come inta L.A. He wants me to get him some heroin. I said, 'What?' I figa'd he wanted to get a whole bunch of heroin so he can give it to somebody and make a ton of money on it.

"He says, 'No. I want it for myself.'"

"What?"

"Yeah, me and Mary," which was his wife at the time, "We got a habit, now."

"What the fuck."

"I don't have no habit. He's got a habit? So he comes out to L.A. Oh, it was unbelievable. We went to Mexico. I scored some heroin in Mexico before I got him the big stuff in L.A. We went on a vacation like for two days. I asked this kid off the street. I mean you talk about stupidity. He sold me this real strong heroin and I 'banged' it. I almost died from it. I mean I was shakin' after a while.

"We were crazy. We went inta this bar. These guys started talkin' shit to us. I'm Italian so it's easy for me to understand Spanish. Next thing you know we're fightin' with five guys. We were punchin' them out. We didn't know nothin' about the laws in Mexico—Jesus Christ, you can go away for twenty years on just a little infraction. If we would'a got arrested, they would'a shaken us down. Who knows what would'a happened."

Coming back in the car Vince started to feel the effects of the heroin, again. "I started to get the shakes real bad. This girl I was with was tryin' to keep me warm. You talk about a cat with nine lives. I had a million lives."

Ironically, Vince always looked up to Mikey. Up until that time, Mikey's life was something Vince envied. "Here's a guy that I usta wanna be like and now he's shootin' dope like it's goin' outta style."

Mikey's life would take an even more dramatic turn for the worst years later.

***

Another time while on vacation in New York, Vince saved his cousin's life. "My cousin Randy and me hung out together all the time when I went back to New York to visit. It was like the movie *High Noon* where Gary Cooper gets off the train, straps on his guns and goes right to the gunfight. I'd get off the fuckin' plane in New York, and instead of goin' to relative's houses, we'd get in the car and go downtown to cop heroin, then shoot up. That was the first thing I'd do. What a life!

"One time, I was there for two weeks, and we're up on a fuckin' rooftop. I shot up and I'm in the 'nod.' All of a sudden, I look up and these two Puerto Ricans, they're gonna throw my cousin off the fuckin' roof. (Fucked up my whole high.) I usta carry these Italian stilettos all the time. So they're ready to throw him off the fuckin' roof, and I pushed the button on the blade, and I stuck it in this Puerto Rican's neck. I said, 'Listen, you know what? If he goes off the roof, you go with him. I'll stick this right through your fuckin' eyeballs. Put him down and get the fuck outta here.

"They ran. They were gonna throw him off the roof 'cause that's what they do in Harlem. Shootin' dope with these 'skivoots' (low-lifes) of Puerto Ricans. Of course, they got us some good shit. So he's ODing. I ran downstairs and knocked on this door. This lady comes to the door. I said, 'Ma'am ya gotta call '911!' There's a guy on the roof. He's dyin'. Ya gotta get him help.'

"And I go back up there to try to revive him. As soon as I heard the sirens, I took off 'cause I was dirty. From a distance, I watched them resuscitate him and he was all right. Then, I saw them get him in the ambulance, and I said, *Fuck, ay, I did a good thing*. So I went back to his apartment and I burglarized it. I took $2000 in cash, jewelry and everything. And I said to him later, 'Listen ya cocksucker. What the fuck. I saved your life.'"

CHAPTER 16

Vince Meets Lydia

In the spring of 1974, I moved to Hollywood where my girlfriend and I shared an apartment on the top floor of an apartment building on Fuller Avenue between Hollywood and Sunset Boulevards. Our apartment overlooked the swimming pool where the local cast of characters that lived in the building hung out. Since I worked a full time job during the week, I didn't get to hang out at the pool except on weekends and holidays. It was on one of those occasions that I met Vince. We hit it off immediately. He lived on the second floor just off the elevator. He and his wife, Cheryl, had recently split up.

When I found out that he cut hair, I started going to his shop on Berendo Street. Vince was a hairstylist to both men and women. Sometimes my girlfriend would have Vince cut her hair as well. It was always an enjoyable experience getting your hair cut by Vince.

Shortly after I met Vince, he met a Mexican girl named Lydia who eventually moved in with him. "I met Lydia Thanksgiving Day. She was staying at my friend's house, and I thought—*Wow!* She had red hair, a beautiful girl. It clicked between us. It was an incredible feelin' right from the start. We were inseparable. The night we met we went to this placed called The Set in Beverly Hills on Doheny and Wilshire. And at the time, I was goin' away for 90-days to Mira Loma Work Camp."

This sentence was the result of the marks charge when Vince overdosed and went to L.A. County Hospital. "I was also facin' a year in county jail for another internal possession charge. I went to court in my own defense, and I beat that one. I'd be cuttin' hair and they'd [the police] walk in on me, and they'd look for marks. They figa'd if they couldn't catch me for dealin', they'd catch me for internal possession. After a while, I started doin' it between my toes."

Not too long after Lydia and Vince started dating, Vince went away to serve his sentence at Mira Loma. "If she had any brains—I mean she had just met me and I was goin' away. But she came to visit me in jail. Then shortly after that, she saw me go to jail again. But she stuck with me. She was a tough one, and tough with me, too. I like that in a woman. She'd listen to me, but yet, she wouldn't put up with any of my bullshit. It turned me on. I was like a tornado with all these women. I just ripped them all up. I was so fucked up. Never satisfied, always lookin' for new women."

Lydia worked in the insurance industry, but you immediately sensed her ambitiousness and a desire to raise herself up from her poor Mexican roots. She had bigger plans for her life than even Vince could imagine. With the same drive Vince had for criminal activities and hairstyling, Lydia had for becoming a successful businesswoman; a route she would pursue and prove to be successful. Her ambition inspired Vince to achieve more and better things for himself: to be a better hairstylist, to acquire more clients, and to own his own shop.

Although Vince and Lydia were obviously passionately in love, their personalities clashed—probably what attracted them to each other. They could easily find something trivial to argue about. For instance at dinner one evening in a Thai restaurant, they had an argument about the quality of the fried rice. Vince said it was good; Lydia said it was soggy or too dry. I don't remember which. We watched and listened in amusement, avoiding getting involved in the argument. These types of heated discussions always made dinner with them an interesting affair.

Even though they easily locked horns, Lydia and Vince had a lot in common. They liked fashionable clothes and lots of them. They loved good food, going out to restaurants and clubs to dance. Vince once told me they were "Bohemians," and over the years, I often kidded him about being a Bohemian.

Arguments were an integral part of their relationship. It seemed to fuel what their relationship was all about. They had many fights at the Fuller Avenue apartment. Unfortunately, they lived directly over the building managers' apartment, a couple of transplanted Southerners. He was pretty harmless, but his wife whose name was Lethal was much more difficult to deal with. So after one of Lydia and Vince's more violent blowouts, Lethal summoned the police to restore order. As a result of the incident, Vince and Lydia were asked to move out of the building. From there they moved to an apartment a block away from the beach in Santa Monica.

Vince continued to use drugs, drink heavily and be involved in illegal activities throughout their turbulent relationship. Then in 1980, they decided to get married.

CHAPTER 17

The Coked-up Hit Man

To Vince's way of thinking he had everything going for him—pockets full of money, a beautiful woman, all the drugs he wanted, plenty of clothes, a well-established hairstyling business and well connected friends. Nevertheless, there was always something missing for him. He always wanted more—more money, more clothes, more women, more drugs, more alcohol.

"One night, my addictions actually saved me. I was hangin' out in the Marina with all my Italian friends."

The Marina area of Los Angeles, just south of Venice on the west side of L.A., is a man-made area that became very popular in the '70s because of the clubs and restaurants adjacent to the pleasure boat docks. The area is also populated with residential apartments and condos that line the surrounding waterfront. The main access route through the Marina is a road that loops from Lincoln Boulevard to the south and back to Lincoln Boulevard on the north.

"Me and my friend Charlie were dealin' cocaine in the loop. So Charlie one night, 'cause I was crazy, says, 'This kid Crazy Al from Palm Springs—he wants a guy hit. You wanna look inta that?'

"What's he givin'?"

"He's givin' twenty large ta do a hit on a drug dealer in the Valley."

"I'll do it."

"Ya wanna do it?"

"Charlie knew where I came from—so he knew I was serious. Charlie calls this kid from Palm Springs. The kid comes up. He says, 'Charlie says you're good people.'"

"Yeah. So whatta we gonna do here."

"A black guy in the Valley, he's fucked me around. I got a '30-06 in the car. I want ya ta waste 'em. Ya can get 'im right through the window of 'is house."

"Great."

"Besides the money, I'll give ya some coke."

"Whatta ya mean by coke?"

"I'll give ya about 15 ounces of coke."

"Awright."

"So on the way out there I start blowin' this coke."

The trip to the San Fernando Valley from the Marina is at least an hour drive without traffic on the freeways. On the freeway, speeds are in excess of 65 miles an hour. From the Marina loop, you have to drive surface streets to the Marina Freeway, then transition to the 405 Freeway North that goes over the Sepulveda Pass, then onto surface streets in the Valley. Add cocaine to the trip and it's a hair-raising journey.

"Here's the problem. You put coke in me. You don't know what's gonna happen. By the time we got out to the Valley, I'm high and I'm like Tom Mix. I'm ready to shoot anybody. Now this kid's gettin' nervous."

This type of reckless behavior is another reason why Vince feels he didn't get made in the mob. "When I was sober, I was cool as a cucumber. Put that shit in me–anything can happen. There's somethin' not workin' right."

"So this guy's drivin' with me and he knows that I'm capable of anything 'cause Charlie told him. But now he's scared and he's not so inta doin' this hit. So we finally get to where we wanted to go in the Valley. I forget exactly where it was. I pull out the gun from the car. He says, 'Look! Look! I changed my mind.'"

"Whatta ya mean ya changed your fuckin' mind?"

"Look, I don't wanna do this. Please. We can't do this."

"Ya drag me out here for nothin'."

"I'll give ya—."

"Ya give me money—ten fuckin' grand, and I want half of that fuckin' coke."

"I'm really gone now, I mean, and my eyes were wild. I'm ready to kill this kid, Al."

"He says, "Please. Please, listen…""

"So he gives me the ten grand, and he's drivin' me back."

Three blocks away from where Vince was to do the hit they pass a Winchell's Donut. There were seven squad cars and eight police motorcycles parked outside. The police were all inside drinkin' coffee.

"We would'a shot that '30-06 three blocks away. You talk about gettin' caught. They would'a swarmed in on us. I call that a Godshot. And what I put that poor girl [Lydia] through. I came home and threw the ten grand on the table. I usta love throwin' money around like that. 'Look at all this coke I got.' She was petrified."

***

No matter how much success Vince achieved in his hairstyling business he just couldn't give up his old ways. He attracted the same type of people as customers and friends that he always had. It was like an insatiable disease for him, another addiction he had to deal with. Who knows whether it was the job or the neighborhood that brought that type of clientele into his barber chair or whether Vince himself attracted them.

"Danny Francesco was a customer, and he was involved with Jimmy DiStephano who was the Mafia boss in L.A. at the time. Danny knew I was a 'stand up guy.' The next thing you know, I'm hangin' out with Danny, and makin' money with him. I'm settin' up burglaries for him. I got him connected with the airline ticket thing where I was sellin' hot airline tickets. I was also sellin' coke and hot credit cards. We had all kinds of scams. We usta hang out in a place called 'Treasures' in the Valley where all the mob guys usta hang out. I was in my glory. I carried a gun again, and once again, I thought I was gonna be made."

This was the same kind of dangerous life Vince left behind in New York, the same type of crazy characters that were psychotic out-of-control guys. Vince put his life on the line again just by hanging out with them.

"We're in this Italian restaurant in the Valley one time, me and Danny. And when Danny would drink he'd get crazy. There was a restaurant, 'Godfrey's.' Danny didn't like the guy who owned it. Ernie Ross was his name. So Danny gets drunk, and he says, 'Ya got your gun with ya?'"

"Yeah."

"Come on we're gonna go down ta Ross's and I'm gonna shoot this motherfucker."

"Danny, you're fuckin' crazy."

"No, this cocksucker—."

"Danny, he's connected."

"I don't give a fuck where he... Fuck him! Are ya with me?"

"Of course, I was with him. So we go down there. And I said to myself, *This is my night to go down*. And I was goin' down with him 'cause I was loyal to him. We get to Godfrey's and we go to open the door to go in—the door's locked. It was closed for the night. I said to myself, *Oh, Madone*. And the next day, once Danny sobered up, he didn't even remember sayin' that he wanted to go."

Vince is convinced that if Godfrey's would have been open that night he would be dead today.

"Years later, I pick up the L.A. Times and fuckin' Danny Francesco ratted out the whole L.A. family. But he didn't mention my name 'cause I was small potatoes. But he 'dropped a dime' on all the wise guys. Who knows the cops or the feds probably had him for something. They also said he was dying of lung cancer or some disease."

CHAPTER 18

Godshots on the Road

For several years Vince had been hanging around with the Mexican girl Lisa and her friends. He and Lisa were dealing and doing drugs together. There was a physical attraction between them, but it had never been consummated.

"Then one night, I finally was gonna pop this broad. She comes inta the fuckin' bedroom with a turban on her head... her robe opens up with a body that was unbelievable... a good lookin' broad. I go on top of her, and I'm gonna fuck her. I nodded out right on top of her. She pushed me off, and said, 'You know that you're a fuckin' disgrace.' So I got up and had a few shots of Jack Daniels, got dressed, and got in my car."

Vince was in Montebello, some 25 miles from his home in Santa Monica. To get home it was mostly freeway driving.

"I had my 1980 Pontiac Firebird about three weeks. I'm goin' down the freeway and I'm high. I konked out, hit the divider and the car was scrapin' along the wall. I was in a blackout when I hit it. I heard this noise and when I looked up, I saw sparks so I stopped the car.

"Now, this is another time that makes me believe God is in my life 'cause this is an insane story. In the rocker panel of the Firebird, I had a '45 and coke. A cop pulls up behind me. The car's against the divider and facin' in the wrong direction. I'm pretty fucked up; that's obvious. The cop gets out of his car and I'm thinkin', *This is it. I'm gone for life.* He said somethin' to me. I said somethin' to him. I had a blowout and this is what I don't understand—the cop started changin' the tire on my car. He took out the spare. The coke was right near it, under the rocker panel. I mean he had to go lookin' for it. You couldn't find it that easily. But he put the good tire on my car. He should'a had me up against the car in handcuffs. Now, this is how sick I was in those days—I got in the car and looked in my rear view mirror and said, *That fuckin' sucker*."

Today, Vince can't make any logical sense out of the incident. When I pressed him about being in a blackout and hallucinating about the whole thing, whether the accident really happened and the cop actually changed his tire, he swears on his mother's grave and his daughter's life that the story is absolutely true. The only explanation that he can offer is that he said something to the policemen that made an impression. The policemen overlooked the fact that he was loaded and helped him. But the events of that night weren't over yet. He still had a long way to go before he would get to Santa Monica.

"After that I'm drivin' down the freeway, and all I kept thinkin' about was my poor car. Not thinkin'—*You're fucked up, man. Your life's a mess. They're gonna put you away*.' No, I didn't think that at all. What dawned on me was—*Oh, my car, it's brand new, and I kept it so nice*. But as I'm drivin', I'm nodding out over and over. I kept tellin' myself all the way home—*Whoa, whoa, wake up, wake up*. Finally, I get off the 10 Freeway at Lincoln Boulevard and I take it all the way to Montana Avenue. I make a left hand turn on Montana. All of sudden I hear an explosion. I must have hit the accelerator of the car just as I nodded out again. I went flyin' through the red light inta the intersection, hit a parked Cadillac that hit a Volkswagen parked in front of it. Thank God no one was near me. My car was like an accordion.

"I felt blood comin' out of my head. My nose was in two pieces. It looked like a peeled banana. I had to pick up part of it. The cops came. Now, I still got the drugs and the gun in the back. Thank God the back of the car wasn't fucked up. It was just the front. The steering wheel was bent and there was blood all over the fuckin' place. There's a bump under my nose now because of that."

Vince had to have microsurgery to fix his nose and he doesn't recall much of what he said to the police. "The fuckin' cop said, 'Well you need help.' I'm fuckin' smashed, and I'm thinkin', *I'm a menace on the road. Ya put handcuffs on me. Ya take me away.* The cops called my wife and she came down in a bathrobe. So, whatta I do? The cop says, 'We'll have it towed for you.'

"No, ya know what? My buddy has a body shop. I'll have it towed and everything. Officers, ya've been so nice to me." I mean I bullshitted them. I called my friend, and he took care of it for me."

Sure the police were nice to him. They should have put him in jail and thrown away the key. Not many people under the influence of drugs or alcohol survive one terrible accident in a night, let alone two. Vince calls it a Godshot. You can call it whatever you want. He's one lucky guy. The fact is, this wasn't the only incident in his life where he should have been seriously injured, killed, or where he could have killed or injured other people. Godshot or not, he seems to have the luck of the Irish, the nine lives of a cat.

CHAPTER 19

With a Little Help from My Friend

After the incident on the freeway and the accident that followed on the Santa Monica street corner, Vince related the story to a customer of his who just happened to be a good friend as well as a psychologist. Vince thought the whole thing quite humorous and shrugged it off nonchalantly with a touch of bravado. Sure, he had cheated death one more time and wasn't sent to jail, either. But his friend was much wiser and perceived a serious problem and wanted to help.

As Vince told his friend the story, his arrogance about the incident showed. His friend wasn't laughing at the parts Vince thought were funny. Instead, he stared back at Vince in the mirror and said, "Vince, I've know you a couple of years now. Can I tell you something?"

"Sure."

"I think you're an alcoholic."

"What? You're outta ya mind, man. I'm not an alcoholic."

"I went in my pocket. I had about 20-grand. I pulled out this fuckin' money. 'Does this look like I'm an alcoholic? Ya go down to Fifth and Main downtown L.A. They got bottles in paper bags stickin' out of their pockets. They look like they haven't eaten in a year. That's an alcoholic, not me.'"

"No, no. Alcoholism is between your ears. I have a good friend, Harvey. He's a counselor. His office is at Fourth and Santa Monica. Why don't you do this? Go down and talk to him. He'll tell you if you're an alcoholic or not."

"Wait, wait. What is this—like a counselin' thing?"

"And, I'm thinkin', *Fuck that*. But once again, I was schemin'."

Vince was thinking about what Lydia would say. She had been living too long with his drinking, drug addiction and philandering.

"She'll think I'm doin' somethin' to help myself. 'Cause she was ready to leave. Oh yeah, she was ready to bolt. We were together about 13 years. It was really bad. Poor kid, she really went through a hell of a lot with me. She became an enabler 'cause she was addicted to me. Enablers do that to alcoholics. She'd say, 'I'm gonna leave.'"

"Yeah?"

"Round one. Twenty rounds later, 'I'm gonna leave you.'"

Vince's customer may very well have been the best friend Vince ever had. He managed to convince him to go see Harvey for an evaluation and surprisingly, Vince went. Harvey asked him, "Do you wanna take a test?"

"Sure."

"There are 20 questions. Can you answer them honestly?"

"Ya got it."

"If you get two wrong, you're an alcoholic, or three wrong, you definitely have a problem."

When Harvey looked at the results of the test, he said, "Boy, you don't have one question in your favor proving you're not an alcoholic."

Vince got all twenty questions wrong.

"He scared me. So, what I did after that—I was smart enough to not drink and drive anymore. But I still drank and did drugs."

Following his meeting with Harvey, Vince joined a group that helped people like himself. Most of the people in the group had received DUIs and were sent there by the courts.

"I wasn't in trouble with the law or anythin' so I went and paid my own way."

Vince finally started to become aware that he had a problem. "It was like a seed was planted in my head to get me inta AA [Alcoholics Anonymous]. I started to change a little bit—just a little bit. I was still doin' drugs. I was still involved with the mob. The mob thing made me feel powerful, strong, 'cause deep down inside I never felt that way. I made people believe that I was a tough guy that I had some kind of power, but I always felt like an imposter. I was a good imposter, too. But I fooled everybody except myself."

Even though Vince attended the group meetings regularly he didn't take them seriously and hadn't gone into AA yet. But somehow the meetings began to affect his subconscious. Slowly but surely, he started to see his abusive behavior for what it was, and what it was doing to his life and his relationship with his wife.

"One day at this alcoholic group this little kid, Sal Fratello, comes in. He was one of the people who usta be in the group and got inta AA. He was in recovery now, and they asked him to come back and speak. That's what they do. The new people see that there's hope with AA 'cause he changed his life.

"That night, he was part of a panel with several other recovering alcoholics. He spoke about his experiences with drug and alcohol abuse. I looked at this guy. Those were the days of 'Don Johnson,' the *Miami Vice* look. That's how I dressed then. I had on this linen jacket, the T-shirt, the whole outfit with the tan and all the bullshit. Sal looks like my twin brother, but he's a short guy. He starts talkin' about his feelin's. Why he started drinkin', and about being in prison in Mexico, and being involved with the boys in Boston. I'm sayin', '*Holy shit.*' But it was the feelin's that got me. How he felt about how he got started with drinkin' and doin' drugs.

"He talked about feelin's of loneliness; feelin's of not being good enough; feelin's of isolation; wantin' to stay by yourself and grandiose feelin's. It was like being grandiose with low self-esteem. I listened and looked at him and thought, *What a cool lookin' guy*. But I was miserable and he was happy. Yeah, I had all the trimmin's, the girls on the side, the money, the clothes, but I was miserable. I was an empty addict. I was workin' from the outside. After he spoke, I went up to him and I asked him, 'What's your gimmick here?'"

"There's no gimmick. You're an Italian kid?'

"Yeah, I'm Italian."

"You're a cool guy. Ya know I'm in AA?"

"Really?"

"Yeah, actually AACA [Alcoholics Anonymous and Cocaine Anonymous]."

"Really. How come you're so happy?"

"Well, 'cause I'm in AACA. We're not a bunch of squares. My buddy, he's my sponsor. He's an Italian guy. He usta be a mob guy."

"And I said to myself, *Whoa! I gotta meet this guy. Maybe I'll meet this guy. Maybe I could make some money with this guy*. That's how my sick mind was at the time."

Vince had met someone that he perceived to be just like himself. But Sal wasn't like Vince. He had changed and Vince saw the difference. It made him think that the 12-step program might help him, too. Even though he was still in denial, he secretly hoped that he could get sober and be as happy as Sal. From that day on, Vince slowly but stubbornly began to deal with his problem and the full extent of that problem.

CHAPTER 20

Livin' Life on Life's Terms

Sal Fratello took Vince to his first Cocaine Anonymous meeting. At that meeting he introduced Vince to Sal's sponsor ex-mob guy, Vito Dante. Of course, Dante was an alias because Vito was in the Federal Witness Protection Program. He was a former member of the Lucchese crime family out of Newark, New Jersey. Vito shot a mob boss, someone he was also related to, while under the influence of cocaine. Fearing for his life, he ratted out friends and family for protection. Vince speculates that someone gave Vito a 'pass' and that's why he was still alive and living in L.A. Vito turned out to be the perfect sponsor for Vince. They had similar backgrounds and Vito knew all about addictions. Vince will always remember that first time that he met Vito.

"I meet this Italian guy with a gravelly voice. He goes, 'Welcome ta AA. How ya doin'? My names Vito Dante.'

"I'm Vince Ciacci."

"What's goin' on?"

"I'm not doin' too good. I'm fuckin' up my life."

Vito knew exactly what Vince was feeling. He had been down that same road himself, and he could easily relate to Vince's background. Back East, they had even hung around with, and done business with, some of the same people.

"That night I started talkin' to him, we talked about the old days. I thought, *Whoa. I know these guys with Genovese and Lucchese*. But he was on a different plane than me. His thing was: you have a problem—12-steps are my recovery. He said to me, 'Vince, you're a good lookin' kid. You're a sharp kid. Are ya happy?'

"And I said, 'Well I got this… And I got that…'"

"But are ya happy?"

"No, I'm not happy."

"Ya don't feel good about yourself. Do ya?"

"Nah."

"That's why ya drink and do drugs and do your little Italian shenanigans. 'Cause ya never felt good about yourself."

This made Vince very uncomfortable and irritated because Vito was seeing right through Vince's street tough demeanor. "Back then, I couldn't talk about myself, and Vito was pokin' raw nerves."

Because he knew the right buttons to push, it only took a few minutes before Vito brought tears to Vince's eyes. Then he said, "I know how ya feel."

"Yeah?"

"Ya want me ta help ya?"

"How ya gonna help me?"

"I'm gonna get ya involved with the 12-steps. Ya willin'?"

"'All right. I'll give it a shot.' I told him. 'But I wasn't really serious about it.'"

As Vince got more involved in the 12-steps program, he began to realize more things about himself. For one thing, he suffered from more than one addictive behavior. Besides Alcoholics Anonymous and Cocaine Anonymous, he also qualified for Sex Anonymous and Narcotics Anonymous. So Vito became Vince's sponsor and began to work with him on a regular basis, although they butted heads every step of the way.

"One day he says to me, 'Ya think you're a real ladies' man. Don't ya?'"

"Ah fuck, ya know how many beautiful girls I been with."

"Let me ask ya somethin'. What did they like about ya?"

126

"And I said, 'Well I'm a good lookin' guy. I'm a tough guy. I'm a money maker.'

"He says, 'Vince, Vince. What lady?... If you had a daughter and she was growin' up, would ya want her to go out with a guy with all the qualifications ya just told me about yourself? Would ya want her ta be with ya?'"

"I choked a little and said, 'No fuckin' way.'"

"Let me ask ya somethin' else. Those girls that ya went out with...'"

"'Oh, ya should have seen some of them.'"

"Right. They were beautiful. I know the routine. What kind of girls were they? What are your qualifications as a man? I mean the ones ya told me—that's not a man. That's a hoodlum. That's a coward. That's not a man.'

"Then I was gettin' angry. He says, 'Aaa, that's all right, get angry. What good qualifications do ya have? What kind of women would go out with a guy 'cause he's got money, he's a tough guy, he's good lookin' and he's crazy? What fuckin' kind of a woman calls ya a ladies' man? That's not a ladies' man. That's a man that attracts lunatics like 'imself.

"Oh, he was gettin' to me. He says, 'And, ya think your a tough guy, don't ya?'

"Yeah, I'm good with my hands."

"Yeah, what kind of a tough guy are ya? You're not a tough guy. You're just a little kid that's scared to death to live life on life's terms."

"Oh, then I got really mad."

"He says, 'That's all right. Get mad. I went through this shit just like you. I was a tough guy too. I'm not a tough guy.'

"I started thinkin' about it. He was peelin' my onion; peelin' away the layers of bullshit and the illusions that I was livin' under. In other words, he was getting to the reality of my life and makin' me see the truth about the way I was livin'."

That was only the beginning of Vito and Vince's relationship. If Vito had been a businessman, a college educated person or anyone else, the relationship would have never worked. Vince related easily to another street guy. But despite their obvious rapport, it wasn't an amicable relationship by any means. Vito didn't trust Vince enough with details about his past because he feared Vince would drop a dime on him if Vince got angry enough with Vito—which he often did. But, as angry as Vince would get with Vito, he would never rat him out. It just wasn't in his nature to do something like that, but Vito took no chances. Vince loved Vito, but the road ahead for Vince would be a difficult one with many starts, setbacks and failures.

CHAPTER 21

My New Friends

With Vito as his sponsor, Vince immersed himself in the 12-Step Program. But it was difficult for him on more than one level. For one thing, Vito really knew how to get under Vince's skin. This led to many arguments between them, and being in the program churned up lots of emotions that Vince didn't know how to deal with. His wife Lydia bore the brunt of most of his frustration.

"I was infuriated with Lydia when I first got sober."

His feelings about Lydia led to even more arguments between him and Vito. Vito was married to a woman named Renee. Vito would often compare his relationship with Renee to Vince and Lydia's relationship, and Vince resented this.

"He didn't work. Renee worked. All he did all day was talk on the phone to people he was sponsorin'. She'd come home at night. She'd cook and put the food on the table. He'd actually say to her, 'Cut my meat for me.' And then, he had the nerve to talk about me and Lydia.

"I said, 'Who the fuck are you to tell me about Lydia? Where do ya get off askin' her [Renee] to cut your meat?' You're gonna compare me and Lydia to you and Renee? What are ya—God or somethin'?' That's how our fights would get started and then we'd get inta it even more. Oh, it was hysterical—our relationship. But that's my personality too. Plus what I came from didn't help. My parents argued all the time, and when I was at home I always argued with them. But I needed a strong sponsor—and he was it."

Vince was sober for only three weeks and struggling to find his way in the program. His cravings for drugs and alcohol were at their worst when something significant happened to him.

"My nerves and everything were raw. Vito says to me, 'I want ya ta come ta this meetin' tonight. There's a guy comin'. Who knows, ya might know 'im. Maybe ya did time with this fuckin' guy.' I go to the meeting and see this guy. He's got a head like a caveman, an ugly fuck with sunken eyes, long stringy hair and fucked up teeth."

Bobby O'Neal was his name and there was something about him that stirred Vince's subconscious. Vince could tell Bobby was a tough guy, but there was somethin' else.

"The minute I saw him I said, *Hey wait, I know this fuckin' guy from somewhere*, but I couldn't place him. Vito said that he was from Italian Harlem. There were a lot of Irish guys up there. Half of the guys up there were either Italian or Irish. So I'm thinkin', *Where do I know him from?*"

So I said to him, 'By the way, do you know my crime partners: Jacky Santo, Danny Kelly?'

"Oh yeah, I know Jacky Santo. I know Kelly."

"So I said to myself, *That's where I know him from.*' Then, when I heard him speak, I couldn't believe the guy did time in places that I did time. It was good to hear that he had straightened out his life 'cause of the program. He was married, had a boat and a good business. He wasn't a crook anymore. I mean this guy usta be a master burglar. The cop, Popeye Doyle from the *French Connection* movie, usta chase this guy over rooftops in New York.

"Hearin' this guy speak, hearin' his story—all of a sudden—I got this hope in me. Where I'm sayin', *Jesus Christ if this fuckin' guy can get sober, anybody can get sober*. There was somethin' else that drew me to him. After the meeting, I couldn't wait to talk to him. I told him things I did. He told me things he did. I did this. He did that, too. And the next mornin' when I woke up, I couldn't wait to call this guy. He gave me his number 'cause you know guys in the program they wanna help other addicts. Especially a New York guy wantin' to help another New York guy.

"So we're talkin' on the phone, and I said, 'Ya know Bobby, I know you. I know you told me you know Jacky Santo. It's fine, but I just feel I know you from somewhere.'"

"Well, ya know, kid, I was like shit. I was all over."

"Yeah, well I was too. 'I was hangin' out on 29th Street, 49th Street, 55th Street, 107th Street, 95th Street, Brooklyn, Queens, wherever there was a bunch a fuckin' money to be made and crumbs to hang out with, I made sure to be there.'

"He says, 'Yeah, ya know what? I hung out on 55th Street.

"Oh, then you know all those guys: Mikey Armone, Joey the Nose, Frankie Gatta, and all them guys... Johnny Paluski (crazy motherfucker polock guy)."

"Oh yeah, I knew 'em. And Fat Carmine."

"Yeah, yeah."

"And he says to me, 'In fact, ya know what? I was married ta a girl on 49th Street. Her name was Vivian.' *Click, click*, my mind went. I stopped talkin', and he stopped talkin'.

"A few years earlier, I was really disgusted with my life. I was married to Lydia. I was fuckin' other broads. I was runnin' dope. I was a real piece of shit, and I remembered this one time I said to Lydia, 'I did somethin' once. I think I saved a guy from killin' his wife.'

"Back in 1955, I was a little punk kid, 14, a skinny little fuckin' 'wop.' I wanted to be with the tough guys, the older guys. Me and some of the older guys parked cars for this restaurant on 49th Street and 1st Avenue. I lived on 51st Street. I hung out with a pretty tough bunch of guys, the 49th Street crew. There was a girl in the neighborhood named Vivian. Vivian was like a 'puton' (whore).' Everybody was fuckin' Vivian. This Irish guy usta come inta the neighborhood. He was loud and drunk all the time, with a beet red face. I told my friend Kenny, 'This fuckin' cocksucker, where does he come off hangin' out in our neighborhood?'

"Kenny smacked me, 'Shut the fuck up! He's goin' out with a girl from the neighborhood.'

"I was just a kid. Kenny and the other guys were all older than me."

One night Vince was parking cars when the same guy came along. As usual, his presence annoyed Vince, but that night Vince sensed something was troubling this Irishman.

"I'm standin' on the corner by myself waitin' to park some cars. This fuckin' guy comes walkin' up to me, and with this Irish brogue asks, 'Where's Vivian? Ya seen where Vivian is?'"

"'I don't know,' I told him. I knew she was probably bangin' somebody in the neighborhood. She was a cunt. But she was married to him. Apparently, they had a fight. I'm lookin' at the gun in his belt. I'm sayin' to myself, *Oh shit, this fuck's drunk and he's gonna kill her*. I don't know what it was. I didn't like this fuckin' guy, but I said to him, 'Let's take a walk.' And I'm scared 'cause I'm 14, I know he's got a gun, and he's a lot older than me. I don't know what it was that made me take that walk up to the schoolyard about two blocks away. I started talkin' to the guy, 'Why do ya wanna shoot her? Why do ya wanna waste your life?' This and that… I hated this fuck and I'm thinkin', *Why am I sayin' this to this guy?* Next thing ya know, he says to me, 'Ya know what kid? No fuckin' broad is worth fuckin' goin' to the chair for.' And he left and I never saw him again."

That day on the phone Vince said to Bobby, "Okay, now step back. I want ya to think about this."

"Wha, wha?"

"Do ya remember when ya were maybe around 24, 25 years old? Do ya remember a skinny little Italian kid takin' ya up to the schoolyard? Ya had a gun in your fuckin' belt, ya were gonna kill your wife, Vivian, and the skinny little kid talked ya outta of it."

"Aah, yeah, oh my God! You were that skinny little prick?"

"I was the skinny little prick."

"He didn't say another word. I didn't say another word. I still get goose bumps talkin' about it. That's a Godshot. But we bonded from that day on."

Vince and Bobby became good friends. Bobby would take Vince fishing and was a big help to Vince on his road to recovery, even though Vince claims Bobby was a pain in the ass.

"You know one thing about this guy, he was one of these guys that if you gave him five cents, he'd ask you for ten. Oh yeah, he loved it if you asked him, 'Ya want somethin'?' He'd never say no. We got in a big fight once. I remember sayin' to him, 'Ya cocksucker. Ya know what? I should'a let ya kill that fuckin' bitch. Ya would'a been in the fuckin' electric chair and I would'a never seen your fuckin' Irish ass again.'"

CHAPTER 22

Hitting Bottom

As the months passed, Vince got more involved in the program. He continued to learn more and more about drug abuse, alcoholism, and the problems that plagued him. Then something happened that would eventually solidify his commitment even further and change his life forever. Vince was a passionate fisherman at the time. He and Lydia went fishing for a couple of days at Lake Arrowhead in the San Bernadino Mountains. Vince still talks about the huge trout they caught that weekend. The beautiful setting and relaxation fired dormant passions within them. Vince asked Lydia, "Did ya bring your diaphragm?"

"You know Vince, I don't need a diaphragm for one—two days."

"'Ah, it's okay.' So, we got inta makin' love."

Upon returning home, the relationship settled back into its same troubled routine, until Lydia came home one night after having a few drinks. "She really let me have it. Told me what she really thought of me—about the kind of person I was. I grabbed her. I wanted to kill her and then I just let her go. I said, '*Ah she's drunk.*' A week later, she tells me she's pregnant after she told me everything but the kitchen sink the week before. And I said to her, 'Ya know, I don't wanna have no kid. Faget about it.'

"But she was adamant 'cause we had an abortion once before. She said, 'Look, I'm gonna have this kid with you or without you.'

"All of a sudden, I thought to myself, '*Ya know, maybe this will save our marriage.*' Yeah, right."

The pregnancy strengthened Vince's resolve about avoiding drinking and drugs. "I got proud that she was pregnant and we went to Vegas on vacation. I began playin' the daddy role and I was really inta it. Eventually, we even went and did Lamaze. I kept tellin' her, 'I hope we have a girl. I want a girl so bad.' Finally, Christina was born, and I loved this kid so much."

Approaching fatherhood with all the enthusiasm of a new father, Vince plunged wholeheartedly into it. "I was really inta changin' the diapers, feedin' her, bathin' her, all the things you do with babies."

As far as saving the marriage, the baby did nothing to help, but by the time the baby was born, Vince had been sober for a year.

"But the fuckin' disease is so powerful that if you're not in recovery and really workin' a good program, that disease is on your shoulder doin' push-ups. Waitin'… just waitin'… just waitin'… like a vulture flyin' overhead. Just waitin' for that right moment, then it comes down and gets you. Vito told me when the baby was born to keep goin' to meetings. I told him on the phone one night, 'Vito, Vito, look, I have a kid now. I got no time for meetings.' Lydia was sittin' on the couch. She looked petrified when she heard me say that.

"He said, 'Ya don't get it, do ya? The alcoholic that you are—the shit ya told me. Ya'll be drinkin' in no time. Faget the kid. The kid! Ya won't have a kid anymore. Ya won't have a job. Ya won't have a wife. Ya won't have anythin'. Ya'll wind up in prison. That's where a guy like ya'll wind up.'

"As he's talkin' I'm holding the phone out. Lydia's on the couch and I'm makin' faces mockin' him, *Mister Know It All*. He had a way of tellin' you somethin' that got under your skin. He would give me advice and I would do it my way, not his way, and he would turn around and say sarcastically, 'Is that right! See I told ya.'

"'Ya cocksucker,' I would say. It usta get me crazy."

"Is that right? he'd say.

"Like he knew. 'Cause he did know. 'Cause he was in the program. He knew what an alcoholic was."

Ten months later, Vito's admonitions proved true. Vince and Lydia had an argument and she left the house.

"I didn't have a VCR in those days. I couldn't even watch a movie. I would fall asleep watchin' TV sometimes, but I'd always get up to change the kid's diaper or feed her. So we had this big fight. The baby is in the little swing-stroller sleepin'. The disease says to me, *You know what Vince? You're workin' so fuckin' hard. You work your ass off. You come home—the maid goes home. You take care of the kid.* 'Cause Lydia worked nights. It was gettin' to be— me and her—we were just livin' for the kid. We were hardly havin' sex anymore. She's workin' her ass off. She'd come home late at night. We'd give the kid a bath at midnight in the little washstand. We'd sponge her down. I loved that. But I was gettin' worn out. So when she went out that night. I said to myself, *What the fuck is with this? Is this what it's all about? I'm not in love with the woman anymore. I don't think I love her. I don't even enjoy havin' sex with her. And all that stuff I usta do—my glamour life. It's over. What the fuck's it all about?*

"When I was drinkin', I usta drink those Manhattans in the can. I said, *Ya know what? I'm gonna go to the liquor store. I'm gonna buy a couple of them. She'll never know the difference.* I hadn't been drinkin' for a year. I came home. I drank those Manhattans. Madone, they hit me like—whoa, whoa.

"Later, Lydia called and said, 'I'm not gonna cook. Whatta you want me to bring home? I'll bring home some food.'

"I said, 'Nah, nah, it's okay. I'm not hungry.' I had those drinks in me so I said to myself Oh, I better brush my teeth. She'll never know. She came home. I'm sittin' on the couch watchin' TV, the kid's sleepin'. The minute she opened the apartment door she looked at me and goes, 'Oh my God, you've been drinkin'.

"I got angry, 'Whatta ya mean I've been drinkin'!' So, now I felt like a cornered rat. I jumped up and I started goin' at her. We had this verbal thing goin'. She was so afraid when she saw me drunk again that she just took off, and left me there with the baby.

"At that point, I thought, *So whatta I got to lose. I've already been drinkin'. The kids still sleepin'*. I said, *Fuck it. I'll go get me some more*. But those first few drinks got me tipsy. I backed out my beautiful car and smashed right into an iron pole in the garage. Now I'm sayin', *Fuck everything'*. I went to the fuckin' liquor store I brought home six more Manhattans in the can and polished them off, too.

"I was drunk as a skunk, sittin' on the couch with the baby in my arms. The kid wakes up. God was workin' with me 'cause I was in a coma already. I had eight of those things in me. I knew I fed her. I knew I changed her. A news show comes on the TV and they're talking about 'The New Mafia,' and who's in the fuckin' thing? A guy I knew from New York. They say he just put a hit on another mob guy. My friend was one of the shooters. I'm watchin' this and they say, 'One of the grim reapers.' And they zoom in on him with a telescopic lens being congratulated by his fellow gang members. I'm goin' to the kid, 'Oh, my God. Christina. Christina. That's daddy's friend.'

"I started watchin' this and I'm flyin'. I called Vito that night—shit faced, and he says, 'I told ya!'

"I called him 'cause I wanted to kill him 'cause he was right when he had told me to keep goin' to meetings. So I called Vito and said, 'I'm gonna kill ya Vito!'

"He said, 'You're only a barber. Go cut some hair!" And he clicked the phone."

Today, Vince uses what Vito told him that night when he introduces himself at AA meetings. "It's a big joke in AA today when I speak. I say, 'My name is Vince—and I'm only a barber.'"

Vito hung up on him and Vince immediately called back and said, 'I'm gonna kill ya, ya bastard. I'm comin' to get ya!'"

Vince kept calling back. He claims he must have called about 25 times and Vito would just hang up on him. As drunk as he was, he wanted to take his frustrations out by killing Vito.

"But I had no gun. I couldn't find one. All I had was a big butcher knife in the kitchen, and I grabbed it. Now, I got this knife in my hand. I would'a never made it out of the garage in the car. I musta been toxic with alcohol. I had a lot of those in my system—one after another. I would'a probably smashed the car inta the garage wall. I got the knife in my hand. I'm lookin' over at the baby. I had forgotten I had her there, and I said to myself, *Oh, I can't go kill him 'cause I have Christina here*. So I put the knife down and took care of the baby and I stayed home."

The next morning, Vince found himself on the bathroom floor. "I was layin' on the floor from the alcohol. I couldn't take it any more. I felt like I was dyin'. I cried my eyes out. I mean I was really fucked up. I called Vito cryin', 'Ya gotta help me!'

"He says in that gruff voice of his, 'If I help ya this time, ya gonna take my directions?'

"Vito, I'm beat. I'm beat. I surrender. I can't do it no more. Would ya sponsor me, again?' This, of course, was after I threathened to kill him the night before.

"And he said, 'Ya gotta listen' ta me.'"

Vince agreed to once again become active in the program and have Vito as his sponsor. But the disease wasn't done with him yet.

"After talking to Vito, I said, *Fuck it, since tomorrow I'm gonna get sober, I might as well get good and drunk now*."

Vince proceeded to drink even more Manhattans. "I almost died. Little Sal Fratello came over to bring me some food, but I couldn't eat nothin'.

"Lydia came back three days later, and found me face down on the bathroom floor. I'd gone to the bathroom, fainted or whatever, and my head was split open, blood everywhere. My face after drinkin' was all puffed up. She came to the bathroom floor, looked at me and said, 'Oh, my God. Look at you! You're gonna die just like your mother did! (Vince's mother had a drinking problem in the later years of her life, and it probably contributed to her death.) I can't take this no more. I'm outta here. I gotta go.'

"I was comin' off of alcoholic poisoning. I had stopped drinkin', but I was so fucked up. Sal Fratello came over with this girl. They call it a '12-Step Call' when you come over to help. He saw how fucked up I was, too. He brought a pizza, but I still couldn't eat."

Most alcoholics hit bottom before they can truly start on the road to recovery. This was the case with Vince. He had hit his bottom.

"I remember Lydia sittin' on the couch, and I'm makin' all these promises and everything. She was determined she was gonna leave and take the baby. Of course, when I got sober I tried my old con game on her. She wouldn't buy it. She said, 'If it was just me I would stay. I'm not gonna raise my daughter in an alcoholic home.'"

Later that night, when Lydia came home, she wouldn't talk to him. She was cold and aloof. Her mind had been made up; her future decided, and Vince wasn't to be a part of it.

"I couldn't get to her anymore. That night I went to sleep, and this is a miracle of God. It's like something [a strong feeling] comes over you that assures you that you've been through the worst and it's all over. I don't know if it was a dream, a vision, or what, but it was so strong. It was like gettin' the winning lotto ticket. I woke Lydia up and told her about it, and she said, 'I'm glad for you. I hope you're right but you've told me so many times before. I'm still leaving.'

"When she left I dove inta the program with everything I had."

Vince got back on the road to recovery with Vito's help, but it was too late for the marriage. Lydia left and never came back and she took the baby with her. Vince became an absentee father with regular visits with Christina. He feels that it was his relationship with his daughter that also helped save his life and kept him from going back to his old ways. After that, life started to change for the better. But his battle with alcohol and drugs was far from over.

Chapter 23

Vince Becomes a Sponsor

"I didn't go inta AA and the lights went on. When I started to get sober it didn't happen overnight, I went in and out, in and out. I wasn't an easy guy to work with, either."

This isn't surprising since none of the good things in Vince's life came easy for him, and when it came to his own emotional well being, things were even more difficult. When he would get angry with his sponsor, Vito, he would lapse back into his old ways. But Vito always remained there for him even during those times when they would argue, curse at each other and call each other names. Vito's stability and conviction would ultimately help Vince return to sobriety. There were also those times when Vince and Vito would be at odds with each other and Vince wouldn't have him as a sponsor. Those were always the most difficult. Vince's addictions would constantly taunt him to take a drink or to do drugs.

"I'm in a CA meeting one night, and I said to myself, *Ya know what? Fuck this program! I'm not stealin' anymore. I'm not makin' money. I'm not gettin' laid. I wanna go home and put on a suit and call my buddies and go out. I wanna start the fuckin' life all over again. I'm sick of this shit. Who gives a fuck. I wanna make a lot of money. I wanna be back. Fuck these stupid motherfuckers in AA and CA. Look at them—they're a bunch of sheep.* But that was the disease talkin'. So I walked outta the meeting. I'm ready to go home. I'm ready to get dressed up, go out and probably kill myself. This kid calls me—'Vince!'

"I turn around, and I see this guy he's about six foot three, he's got hair down to his shoulders with a Fu Manchu mustache. He looks really weird to me. I said (arrogantly), 'Yeah?'"

"Are you Vince?"

"Yeah. I'm Vince."

"Can I talk to you?"

"'Yeah. Whatta ya want?' *I'm a man with a mission here,* I'm thinkin."

"Look, you don't know me, but would you sponsor me?"

"My first thought was: *Sponsor ya? I'm lookin' to get fuckin' loaded. I'm gonna fuckin' get drunk. Ya want me to sponsor ya?* 'Why'da ya want me ta sponsor ya?'"

"Because I like the way you carry yourself. I just feel you would be a good sponsor. Would you help me?"

"Fuck! Nobody ever said that to me in my whole life, 'Would you help me?' Because I felt I wasn't important enough for anybody to want anythin' that I had. Now, all of a sudden something happened in my mind. I looked at the kid like, *What a jerk-off this kid is.* Let's face it, at that time there were not a lotta guys in the program that I would'a hung out with for five minutes, but they were sober. You're not supposed to look at it like you're better than them, but I thought, *I'm a classy guy. Look at these jerk-offs.* I said, 'Whattsa matter?' I tried to act like I knew what I was talkin' about.

"So he says, 'Can we talk?'"

"Sure."

"We wound up goin' for coffee and talkin' for five hours. I didn't drink and I didn't do any drugs like I had planned to do."

At this point in the recovery process something really started to happen to Vince. Vito was not his sponsor, and he met someone that wanted Vince to sponsor him. Vince had no idea what that entailed. He had never sponsored anyone.

"Vito had worked the steps with many guys. I never worked the steps with anybody. The next day I called Vito, and said, 'Vito! This fuckin' kid wants me to sponsor him. I was gonna go out and get loaded.'"

"Yeah, ya fuck. I understand."

"Yeah, but this kid wants me to sponsor him."

"The kid asked ya ta sponsor 'im?"

"Yeah."

"So sponsor 'im!"

"Sponsor him? How the fuck am I gonna sponsor him'? I don't know how to sponsor nobody'."

Vito knew what a great breakthrough this could be for Vince, and he offered to help. This turned out to be a godsend for Vince and his own road to recovery.

"This kid went to three fuckin' meetings a day. He took commitments at every meeting."

Commitments in 12-step programs are tasks that an individual takes on. It could be as simple as making a pot of coffee for the meeting, setting up chairs, handing out literature or preparing reports. Vince was so impressed with the guy's determination and dedication that it began to change his own attitude.

"My ego was sayin', *Wait a minute. This fuckin' kid is doin' all this.* I started goin' to meetings every day. I started takin' commitments, and then Vito and me got back on track again. I started to like workin' the steps over again with him.

"This kid looked up to me, and actually became my role model, but he didn't know it. He was a pain in the ass, too. I gotta tell you. He'd call me three, four times a day. I took him through the steps, and all of a sudden we got closer and became good friends. But I had to be cool 'cause I was supposed to be sharper than him. Every time he'd ask me somethin', if I didn't know the answer, I'd call Vito."

The kid, whose name is Rico, was employed as a head grip at the studios. This was a well paying job that earned him over two hundred thousand dollars a year. The problem was that he couldn't stay away from the cocaine that was so rampant in the movie industry at the time. After his first year of sobriety, he quit his job and got involved with the Boy's Club in Santa Monica where he taught underprivileged kids how to play basketball. Seeing the profound affect Vince had on Rico's life made an impression on Vince.

"This made me feel like I had a worthwhile purpose in life. I said to myself, *What the fuck! This kid can do all this.* The next thing you know I took a panel. A panel is when you go speak in a hospital or you go talk at a prison, or whatever. You share your story 'cause you wanna help other people, maybe even—'plant the seed'—it's called. So I go to the panel at this hospital in Century City and what happens? A kid there likes me—asks me to sponsor him. Now, I got two guys I'm sponsorin'. I'm takin' them through the steps. Then I go to a meetin' one night and another kid asks me to sponsor him. Now, I'm really breakin' my balls here. Before you know it, I got two years in the program and I'm sponsorin' five, six guys. I'm getting respect like you wouldn't believe."

For the first time in Vince's life, he began to have some self-esteem. The night Rico asked Vince to sponsor him was the turning point in Vince's life. It was too late to save his marriage. He and Lydia eventually got divorced, but he still had his daughter to think about. She was living in the San Fernando Valley with Lydia.

"I really wanted to stay sober 'cause of Christina. But when I was leavin' that meeting that night I was gonna go get fucked up, and then my whole life changed for the better."

Chapter 24

Last Temptation of Vince

A year had gone by and Vince, for the first time in his adult life, was still sober. Clean as a whistle, no drugs, no alcohol. He was becoming an honest person with himself and others. It had been a long treacherous journey. There were many Godshots that kept him alive throughout his life. The longer he was sober the more grateful he became that he was still alive. His new life revolved around the 12-steps that he learned to embrace and everyday he became more involved in the program. This helped him to better understand himself and his problems. At meetings, he took commitments and was asked by more and more people to be their sponsor.

"It was like a cake. The ingredients were: go to meetings, take commitments, work the steps, sponsor people and your life starts to change for the better. What you're doin' is givin' back what was given to you. And fuck, I should be givin' back. You talk about justice. If you put all the fuckin' crime I committed on the roster, and you gave me a sentence, I'd have to have 50 grandkids doin' my time for me. So you get grateful. It's funny the people with the most fucked up lives before they get inta the program become the best in the program. It's funny how that happens. It's like they say, 'God takes the dregs of society and makes them his soldiers.'"

That's what Vince became—a soldier. Not only was he working on his own life but he started to affect the lives of others. And with each individual he helped, it made him a better person.

"What I did that really helped me—I took a panel down in a woman's shelter."

147

This was the same kind of panel that Vince attended when he met Sal Fratello that eventually led him to AA. On the panel, Vince shared his story of what his life was like on drugs and alcohol, and how his life had changed for the better without them.

"What I would do is go down there with about three or four girls that had a lot of time in the program. I would lead the panel. Most of the girls at the meeting were there because their husband beat them up or maybe they had a drug or drinkin' problem. When they would hear the girls with me talk about how they changed their lives, it gave them hope. And you'd be surprised how many girls I saw down in that shelter that looked like they were down and out. They got inta the program and did the 12-steps. You see them three, four years later and they got a business suit on. They changed their lives. They got a good job. Then they meet me at meetings and they say, 'Don't you remember me Vince?' And to be honest, I never remember any of them 'cause they looked like scabs when I met them, and now they're all dressed up and ya say, *Whoa!* Everytime that happens, it makes me feel good to know I touched somebody's life. And maybe it was something I said, or something one of the girls that I took down there said that made them see the light. You can be at a meeting and hear somebody say something that makes sense to you, and say to yourself, *Hey, that's me. Or, I can do that.* That's how AA works."

But Vince's journey into sobriety was far from over. His past life would come back to tempt his resolve from time to time. Once he was paid a visit from his old Cuban drug connection, Manny. But this time Vince was sober and Manny was not the person he once enjoyed seeing and for obvious reasons.

"Everytime Manny would call I would love it. I'd cut his hair and his tip would be a big chunk of cocaine, the size of a baseball—pure cocaine. I'd cut it up, grind it to powder, and cut it inta little fuckin' grams. It was worth maybe $1000. So I was sober a year and a half. This was a tough one. He calls me from Miami, 'Hey Vince, this is Manny. Hey, I wanna come get a haircut, man. I ain't seen ya for a long time.' My heart started beatin' faster 'cause everytime he usta call I usta say to myself, *Yes!* Then I'd make sure I had all these little gram size bottles. To me it was paradise. I knew right away I'd be dealin'.

"So he comes out. This was when I had my own joint with Lucille."

Lucille was a French woman that Vince became partners with in an upscale hairstyling salon on a fashionable street in Brentwood.

"Manny comes in with his new wife, a gorgeous Cuban broad. This guy's been married like nine times. I'm cuttin' his hair, and she turns around and says, 'I got a proposition for you.'"

"I said, 'What is it?'"

"'I'm gonna open a hairstyling salon in Miami, and I'm gonna make it into a palace—a Taj Mahal. I want you to be the head of it 'cause you're a great haircutter. But it's a front for our operation. You'll have all the women you want, all the drugs, all the money, and you know the boys down there they'll be tippin' you real big.'"

For the old Vince this would have been the opportunity of a lifetime, something he would not have even given a second thought, but now things were different.

"For a split second, I had forgotten that I had a daughter, and for a split second I had forgotten that I was sober. All I could think was: *Wow! Fuck!* And then it hit me. I'm sober, and I got a daughter, and my life ain't like that no more. I actually had tears in my eyes. She saw my reaction and said, 'Whatsa matter?'

"I respect ya. 'Specially that ya think of me so highly to do this, but I have to decline.'"

"She said, 'This is an opportunity of a lifetime.'"

"Ya don't understand, I changed my life. I'm in AA now."

"And Manny goes, 'Aaa, you're in AA, man. Ya know, my fuckin' guy…' Lookin' at her, he says, 'My man, Papo, down in fuckin' Miami. He does the fuckin' 12-steps. The same shit, man. Ya know man—I respect ya fer that. I respect ya fer that. I respect ya. Ya know what?' He says to her in Spanish, 'Come on!' Like faget about it."

"And she says, 'Mah, Manny…'"

"He says, 'Aaa!' Then he made some kind of hand gesture, meaning to say, *Enough!* That put an end to the conversation. He was a tough Cuban street guy. Then, he turned around to me with a hunk of cocaine in his hand, and said, 'Hey, what am I gonna do with your tip here?'

"And I looked at that fuckin' chunk of coke, and my mind said, *Well maybe I should sell it. Maybe… And I said, no, ya can't touch it—you're sober today.* We're talkin' about a $1000 tip. It was so hard to say no to that. When he left the shop, I felt like a woman who I loved all my life was leavin' me forever, and I was ready to almost call his name, and I stopped. I had these desperate feelin's. But I told myself, *No! You're sober today*, and I smiled and said. *Besides that ya want your daughter to be proud of ya some day.* So once again she saved my life, my kid, 'cause I would'a gone with Manny to Miami."

As it turned out, Vince made the right decision for more reasons than he thought. A year or two later, Manny's Taj Mahal of a hairstyling salon got shot up by the authorities. They were all arrested, and Manny's doing life in prison. Vince considers this another Godshot in his life and another step in his recovery.

Chapter 25

Sober for Life

For the next eight years, Vince continued to chair the same panel at the women's shelter. He worked his program diligently and remained sober despite life continually testing his resolve. He had to deal with the difficulties of joint custody of his daughter and being an absentee parent, often locking horns with his ex-wife. For the first time, Vince was living life on life's terms, and he wasn't scared to live it without drugs or alcohol.

During this same period, his aged father with whom Vince never had a great relationship, lost his life's savings gambling and became more dependent on Vince for his well being and support. Eventually, Vince had to move his father from New York to L.A. where he could take better care of him. His father continued to verbally abuse Vince as he had done so often throughout Vince's life. In his father's eyes, being in AA was a disgrace and not something to be proud of. He was not very supportive of Vince's determination to stay sober.

When Vince's friend from AA, Bobby O'Neil, met Vince's father he told him, "Ya know, Mister Ciacci, you're son may have been somethin' else, but man, this guy—he changed. He really changed."

"And of course, my father wasn't convinced. Maybe he never forgot the time when I was high on drugs and I pulled a gun out on him. I put it behind his head. I told him I was gonna kill him. Ya know ya get so fucked up on drugs and maybe something came up in my mind. Maybe it was something he did to me as a kid.

151

"My father told Bobby about that. Bobby says to him, 'See, nobody understands an alcoholic like another alcoholic. Ya know, Mister Ciacci, ya gotta understand this fuckin' disease is terrible. It turns nice guys inta animals. They do crazy things. Most of the guys in prison taday, ninety-eight percent of 'em, are there 'cause they were drunk, or they were doin' drugs when they committed the crime.' But it didn't do nothin' to change my father's mind."

Throughout Vince's life, he made a lot of wrong decisions. There are those crossroads we all come to in life—you should have gone right but went left. Vince seemed to always go the wrong way, sometimes intentionally, sometimes unintentionally. When Ringman advised him to become a cook in a restaurant when he was released from Coxsackie, Vince should have taken the advice. Unfortunately, many of the paths he chose led to more trouble. Becoming a hairstylist was a good decision for him. It gave him a life's work that he could love, enjoy and take pride in. Joining AA was an action that led him to a better life. Finally, he was on the right path, a good path and nothing was going to sway him. He was still being tested every step of the way. But Vince has learned to live life like the rest of us.

Eventually, the deaths of his close friends, some of them the same people that helped him into AA and to stay sober, would have a profound effect upon him, especially the terrible death of his friend Mikey Bonacorso from AIDS.

"I usta wish I could be like Mikey. When I usta go to Mikey and Mary's house in Astoria, I usta see the big Christmas tree, the family. I'd say to myself, *Look at me. I got nothin' and these guys got everything. Why me?* And it turns out Mikey and Mary wound up shootin' dope like it was goin' outta style. Then, I find out that Mikey broke up with Mary, and he's with this broad in Tennessee, some barmaid that usta work for him. He finds out he's got AIDS from shootin' up with a dirty needle. Not only does he have it, but he gave it to Mary. In Tennessee, he goes and pulls a stickup in a fuckin' drugstore. He was so weak from the AIDS that he had the gun in his hand... this old druggist, pulled the gun right out of his hand and they arrested him. He died in a prison hospital in Tennessee with AIDS. You talk about a lonely death.

"His wife called to tell me about Mikey dyin'. At first, she was surprised to hear my voice 'cause she thought I was dead, too. She was so happy I got sober. She cried and said to me, 'Oh, thank God you're alright, and then she said, I gotta tell ya something.' She told me about Mikey, and that she had AIDS too. That's when I cried 'cause I loved that girl; she was like my sister. But she straightened up her act—no more drugs, but it was too late—she wound up dyin' from AIDS, too.

"I stay in touch with their kids. They're like my Godkids to me. Mikey Junior, he's a good clean-cut kid. In fact, the kid's a boxer and he looks just like his father, but the complete opposite from his father in the way he lives... no drugs, alcohol or crime. He comes out to L.A. every once in a while and we hang out. Nina, the daughter, is a schoolteacher. Thank God they're both doin' good, but there has to be some fucked up scars inside those kids."

Sal Fratello, who helped Vince so much in his early days of recovery, died unexpectedly from a heart attack in 2000. He died way too young, the result of all the drugs and alcohol he'd consumed in his life. Vince took Sal's place as a drug counselor.

Vince's sponsor Vito Dante also died at an early age, also from AIDS. "He got sober and three years later he's helpin' people and he finds out he has AIDS from shootin' drugs with a dirty needle. Vito was a man of honor in the program. When he died he was forty something years old. They did a eulogy for him like he was a Pope. Vito and I really got into some heavy shit. We'd fight—slam the phone down on each other. I didn't know he had AIDS, and I really gave him a rough time. I motherfucked him by talkin' behind his back. Oh, I hated him sometimes. But I loved that guy, loved him and hated him. What a piece of work he was.

"Renee Dante, his wife, is my good friend today. I became her sponsor after Vito died. That's how strong a program she thought I was workin' that she asked me to be her sponsor. And she had more time in the program than me. Here's a girl that sponsors half of the girls in Cocaine Anonymous in L.A., and she wanted me to be her sponsor. To me that's an honor."

Vince's other friend, Bobby O'Neil, died at a young age from Lupus. "I was really proud to be part of Bobby's life. I shared at a big meeting what he did for me. He was like a guru to me. I also shared the story from when I was a kid, and how I kept Bobby from killin' his wife. It makes me feel good to know, even in my insanity, that I was part of helpin' him with his life. It's things like that keeps me goin' in the program.

"So that's why I'm real grateful today that I'm sober. I got a good life and I help people today instead of hurtin' them."

EPILOGUE

Vince has been sober for over twenty-five years. AA worked for him and the 12-steps were like a miracle. After his initial recidivism, he settled into the program and never fell back into his old ways.

"Now I say, 'God is doin' somethin' to help me. God has a plan for me.' All along he has pulled me out of one mess after another," until Vince was finally led to AA. Today, there's a purpose to his life.

Since he has been sober, many things have changed for him. He has learned to get by on a workingman's salary, instead of money from crime. Gone are the wads of cash in his pocket from illegal ventures. The scams and criminal activities have been replaced with good deeds and honest work. Hairstyling continues to be the sustaining force in his life. For many years, he has had the same loyal clientele, and with his winning ways, he still attracts new customers. Despite all the positive changes in his life, things haven't gotten any easier for him. It's how he has learned to deal with them that changed. His father passed away as we began writing this book. In his father's declining years, father and son were actually at peace with each other for the first time.

When his daughter became a teenager, the closeness he once shared with her changed dramatically. Father and daughter had their differences that they have been able to work out over the years. She has grown into a beautiful young woman with her own life now.

Vince's involvement in AA as a counselor and sponsor continues to give him strength. "Today, I'm a man of service. I can go inta any meeting and sometimes I feel guilty the way they act towards me. I always had a hard time when people said something good about me, even today. People raise their hands and say things like, 'If it wasn't for

Vince...' 'Vince helped me...' 'My life was going downhill until Vince became my sponsor.' I feel all clammy when that happens. I'm just tryin' to stay sober. I don't want recognition, but it has really helped my self-esteem."

This is so unlike what life used to be for him. He constantly sought acceptance and most of the time it was the wrong kind of acceptance from the wrong people. As a young boy growing up in the streets of New York, he had very little self-esteem. His only ambition was to be a major criminal. Then, throughout most of his adult life, self-esteem continued to elude him. He wanted to be a made-man in the Mafia, but drugs and alcohol may very well have kept that from happening. This was probably a good thing because that lifestyle demoralized him.

"In my heart, I always felt like I was a good person. Today, I know I am. There's no doubt about it. But even today—I still feel like I always gotta prove myself. I don't like to make mistakes. I like to be right. I like to do good things. After I do them, it makes me feel good. AA made me accepting and tolerant. I learned to overlook faults in other people. Before, I'd act like a human being until you did something that annoyed me, then I'd attack you. Today, I don't do that. I see people differently. How do I know how they feel? How do I know how they think? I don't know unless I walk a mile in their shoes. I'm just so much more accepting today."

Vince recognizes that the people he used to surround himself with were not friends. They called themselves friends but they always had ulterior motives.

"The people I have in my life today I know are there for me. Real people. Good people. Not hoodlums or gangsters judging their friendship according to how much money I make, and how crazy I am. Today I still like the things I usta like."

Vince still enjoys gangster movies, and books about the mob. He even knows some mob figures.

"But it's not who I am. Today I work from the inside. It's a spiritual involvement. It's having a higher power in your life. Where the higher power is inside of you and it controls your whole aura. In other words, you never feel lonely 'cause this higher power is with you. Who, by the way, I call Jesus Christ—my Father in heaven. Not the same Jesus Christ that I learned about in religious instruction in Catholic school. He loves me and wants good for me. All He wants me to do is—his will. Everything that I did before was the complete opposite of his will. Today dishonesty is replaced by honesty—and I'm considerate of other people."

Vince made restitution to many of the people he hurt in the past. Vince repaid his cousin for the jewelry and cash that he robbed from his apartment after he saved his cousin from overdosing. He made amends to his ex-wife, Lydia, by telling her what a terrible husband he was and offered to do anything to help her. He also wrote a letter of forgiveness to his deceased mother and burned it. He had a heart-to-heart talk with his father, and said he could have been a better son, and his father told him he could have been a better father. These were a few of the people he had harmed and he made direct amends to them. This was one of the 12-steps he was taught to live by.

AA also helped him realize what was wrong with the way he looked at life. "You change in the program not by your thinking, but by your actions. You do good actions and they bring good thoughts, and if you do good things you get good self-esteem."

Somehow Vince survived the life he lived and got to where he is today. Call it what you want—Godshots as Vince does—or just plain luck. He didn't become a made-man as he once desired, but he "made it" in life. He has faults, and who doesn't. But he's aware of them, and instead of denying his faults, he works to improve himself. He's open to criticism, and readily accepts help from those willing to offer it.

Vince, like most recovering alcoholics, can still talk fondly about the highs he used to experience under the influence of alcohol and drugs, but the closest he comes to indulging in these vices is in his dreams.

"They call it God's way of givin' you a free high. Oh yeah, I dream of shootin' dope. I dream that I'm drinkin', and then in the dream I hear a voice that says I'm lying about my sobriety, but I'm not. Then I wake up and I don't know if I'm sober or drunk. But I realize it was just a dream. Oh, some of them are very real. I also dream of gettin' shot. Some of my dreams are like the wild, wild, west. When I was really doin' those things, I never dreamt. Somebody said to me, 'This is good you dream about it. You filter these things through your dreams and you don't do them.'"

Vince told me a story about visiting some mob guys he knows. "I went over to their house. There was lots of cocaine on the table. If that was me 20 years ago, I would'a had a plan, put it together with these guys and we would'a executed it. 'Cause my mind was always workin'. You got lemons, you make lemonade. I always wanted to do something criminal. I was addicted to crime and rage. That was me. You give me a little criminal intent I'll make it inta something. 'Cause I was good at thinkin' up crimes. Especially when I did that powder. But those days are over. I'm content and grateful for everything I have. I'm not lookin' for more. I'm grateful for whatever God puts in my life today. I'm still a little crazy... I know that. But I gotta be honest. Even though I don't do the shit I usta do no more, I still glorify it. I still like watchin' it. I still like readin' about it.

"In Bombay, they got these mastodon elephants. They use them for construction. They're monsters, and they breed them, these large elephants. When they're little, they're full of feistiness and pep. So the handlers take this big fuckin' chain with a clamp, and they put it around the elephant's leg, and they take this stake and drive it inta the fuckin' ground and tie the chain to it. There's no way in hell that the fuckin' elephant can get away. The elephant pulls, and pushes, and pulls. But he knows that that stake is in the ground with that chain and it only gives him a certain perimeter to go round and round. He can't go any further than that. So as the elephant gets bigger, he can knock down buildings. And whatta they do? They tie a little rope around his leg at night, and they tie it to a little stick that they put it in the ground. This elephant can just move his leg a little and pull the stick out and just walk away, but he never does. He knows deep down inside that he can only go so far.

"I feel like that elephant a lot of times. Where I think, *You know, I got great ideas. I can do this and that.* Yet inside, I think, *Ah, you're still the same fuckin' guy you always usta be.* But I know I'm not that guy no more."

ACKNOWLEDGEMENTS

I am grateful to Vince Ciacci for entrusting me with his life story. Writing and completing this book gave me the confidence and incentive to finish my first novel, *Railway Avenue*, and then to go on to put this book into publication.

I have to thank my wife, Anita, for her patience and support over the years. Not only has she read and edited my work endless times, but she also put up with my crankiness and frustration during the process. I couldn't have completed this without her.

I would also like to thank Tootsie Schreiber for her support and invaluable editing that helped me to polish this work. And I'd like to thank Bill Carter for his legal advice.

Of course, I wouldn't be in this position today if not for my friends and fellow writers in my writing group who challenged me along the way, read chapters, read the completed work and pushed me to keep making it better. Thank you: Betty Barkman, Barbara M. Crawford, Sandy Cortner, Betsy Janney, Mike Keith, Sheila Davis and Marcie Telander.

In addition, I have to thank the folks who read the completed work, provided feedback and moral support. Thanks to my daughter, Deborah Sanquiche, Harvey Castro, Kim Masters, Michael Frenchman, Al Costanzo, Aggie Jordan, Kathleen Mary, Robyn Zimmerman, Lynda Jackson, Patty Kingbaker and Steve Evans. Also thanks to Jane Thomas, Debra Reich, Sonda Donovan, Jen Hillebrandt, Maria Fenerty, Joan Ham and Nancy Trimm. The writers would like to thank Dick Lippin for his interest in and help with *Almost A Wiseguy*. We are also grateful to the late, Ned Tannen whose support for this project meant a lot.

ABOUT THE AUTHOR

Bob Puglisi has had a varied background from computer programmer to technical writer, actor, screenwriter, playwright, producer, and librarian at the Old Rock Library in Crested Butte, Colorado. In the IT industry, he wrote close to 100 technical manuals and training classes for major corporations.

He has had his stage plays produced in Los Angeles and his hometown of Crested Butte. He has also written a number of full-length screenplays. In 2000, he received a fellowship from the Colorado Council on the Arts for his screenplay *Big White Bonneville*, which he produced as a short film entitled *My Bonneville* that toured the film festival circuit around the country.

His first novel, *Railway Avenue*, is a riveting story about a Vietnam vet, Tommy DiNardo, who returns to Corona, New York, from the war to find his friend and love of his life since he was a five-year-old, in an abusive marriage. Tommy grows up in a neighborhood where neighbors are relatives and friends who depend on each other for support. The characters will live in your mind for weeks after reading the novel.

Bob's acting credits include stage, film and television. Some of his memorable TV roles were on *Matlock* with Andy Griffith, *Hill Street Blues*, and *The Tonight Show* with Jay Leno.

Made in the USA
Charleston, SC
25 May 2014